FINANCIAL TIMES
MANAGEMENT

Knowledge

University of North ...Newcastle

Financial Times Management is designed to deliver the knowledge, skills, and understanding that will enable students, managers and organizations in achieving their ambitions, meeting their needs, wherever they are.

Financial Times Management, is the leading publisher for professionals and students in business and finance, bringing cutting-edge thinking and best practice to a global market.

To find out more about Financial Times Management and Financial Times Pitman Publishing, visit our website at:

www.ftmanagement.com

SCHOOL LEADERSHIP AND MANAGEMENT SERIES

Series Editors: Brent Davies and John West-Burnham

Other titles in the series:

Effective Learning in Schools
by Christopher Bowring-Carr and John West-Burnham

Middle Management in Schools
by Sonia Blandford

Reengineering and Total Quality in Schools
by Brent Davies and John West-Burnham

Resource Management in Schools
by Sonia Blandford

Strategic Marketing for Schools
by Brent Davies and Linda Ellison

Forthcoming title:

Human Resource Management for Effective Schools
by John O'Neill and John West-Burnham

Leadership and Professional Development in Schools
■ ■ ■

How to Promote Techniques for Effective Professional Learning

JOHN WEST-BURNHAM AND
FERGUS O'SULLIVAN

FINANCIAL TIMES
PITMAN PUBLISHING

LONDON · HONG KONG · JOHANNESBURG
MELBOURNE · SINGAPORE · WASHINGTON DC

FINANCIAL TIMES MANAGEMENT
128 Long Acre, London WC2E 9AN
Tel: +44 (0) 171 447 2000
Fax: +44 (0) 171 240 5771
Website: www.ftmanagement.com

A Division of Financial Times Professional Limited

First published in Great Britain in 1998

ISBN 0 273 62409 1

British Library Cataloguing in Publication Data
A CIP catalogue record for this book can be obtained from the British Library

10 9 8 7 6 5 4 3 2 1

Typeset by Phoenix Photosetting, Chatham, Kent
Printed and bound in Great Britain by Redwood Books, Trowbridge, Wiltshire

The Publishers' policy is to use paper manufactured from sustainable forests.

Contents

■ ■ ■

Introduction

■ ■ ■

This book emerges from over 50 years' combined experience in education as the recipients and providers of professional development. We never cease to be amazed at the professionalism, dedication and commitment of the teachers with whom we are privileged to work. This book is dedicated to the thousands who have worked with us, hopefully benefiting from our programmes, but all contributing to our thinking and understanding.

The past ten years have seen a profound and fundamental shift in the role and status of professional development in schools. It has been transformed from a marginal activity sustained by enthusiastic amateurism to what is often highly sophisticated provision comparable with the best practice in any organisation. Our involvement in professional development convinces us that the time is now approaching when the fundamental concepts of professional development have to be challenged. The changing environment that schools are having to operate in, the increased demands on them and new understanding of how we learn require that the fundamental premises of INSET are reviewed and justified.

Most significant is the notion of adults in schools as learners. The concept of the learning organisation is becoming increasingly understood. The means by which adults learn is still elusive but there is enough evidence to allow us to propose new approaches with confidence. An important principle is that the way in which the adults in a school learn is the most powerful model for how young people learn. It is on this basis that we offer this book as a contribution to the debate on the transition from INSET and Baker Days to fully systematic professional learning.

The case studies in Chapter 8 are condensed from original sources and we are greatly indebted to Muriel George, John Ley, Veronica Chalmers, Wiel Veugelers, Henk Zijlstra, Jeff Jones, Pauline Hughes, Iris Geva-May and Yehudit Dori. We would also like to thank Lincolnshire County Council for permission to use material from the Small Schools Project in Case Study 1 and the In-Service and Professional Development Association for permission to include the last three case studies, which appeared in the *British Journal of In-Service Education*.

Thanks are also due to John Wiley & Sons Inc. for permission to use Figure 1.6 and Addison Wesley Longman Limited for Figures 2.4–2.7 and 9.2.

We are very grateful to our colleagues at the International Educational Leadership Centre, Lincoln University campus, and to Brent Davies and

Angela Thody for their continuing advice and support. We are also grateful to Geraldine Bristow, Maureen Young and Debbie Wright for their work in preparing the manuscript.

John West-Burnham and Fergus O'Sullivan

PART ONE

■ ■ ■

Tensions and Challenges in Professional Learning

1
■ ■ ■

Professional Development –
An Overview of the Issues

Introduction

This book represents a bringing together of two significant strands in continuing professional development and our understanding of the ways in which organisations (including schools) respond to increasingly rapidly changing contexts in contemporary society. The focus of the book will be on learning itself, both the individual learning of teachers (and how this can add value to the experience of pupils and students in schools) and the teams and organisations in which individuals learn as a group seeking to build a learning organisation.

The first strand is that of continuing professional development (CPD) itself and developments in the structure of (in-service education and training) INSET and CPD for the teaching profession. Although this is covered briefly in the next section (and in much more detail in a number of recent texts such as Glover and Law (1996)), it is appropriate to set the scene for this discussion. The Teacher Training Agency (TTA) has built up a good head of steam in developing a coherent framework for CPD in the teaching profession in the last two years and, although there is a healthy scepticism as to the long-term effects of the proposals (see, for example, Graham, 1996), in general attention being paid to the life-long learning opportunities for teachers can only be regarded as a 'good thing'.

The second strand concerns a deeper level of organisational and individual development. It has become a truism to talk about refocusing from content in the curriculum to skills and competencies as a way of coping with rapidly changing knowledge. Even when those of us in the middle years of our careers started in the business of teaching and learning, the way to 'get on' was to select a narrow field of enquiry and become an 'expert' in that area, or,

3

alternatively, move into management as soon as possible to avoid having to learn at all! Nowadays, it is impossible to know everything about anything, so the focus on learning itself and in imparting skills of knowledge acquisition, management and use enables today's students to enter the wider world better equipped to respond to the challenges of tomorrow.

However, this requires a fundamental shift in the way in which we think about organisational structures and development. There is currently a similar rethinking going on in the natural sciences (Capra, 1997). Newtonian physics enabled the landing of men on the moon (and their return) though the full power of Einsteinian thinking is only just being explored in fields such as chaos and complexity theory. In nuclear physics, scientists are beginning to lose interest in chasing down more (smaller and increasingly transient) particles and are focusing on the interactions of forces and the transformation of matter into energy and vice versa.

In human resource management, it is ironic that often the first response to failures in the system is to concentrate on structures and outputs (cf. National Curriculum, Appraisal, GCSE, League Tables, etc.). Perhaps it is because these aspects are easier to understand and fix. Instead of treating the symptoms, a more effective approach is to understand the process. This is the organisational equivalent of the shift away from facts and towards skills in individual CPD. However, it is not just moving from a content/product focus to a skills/process one, it is also adopting a stance which is reflective and reflexive. That is not only learning new skills and competencies (in place of more and more facts) but also learning how we do this – in short, learning how to learn.

In this book we hope to tackle this through identifying and discussing the key issues in individual and organisational learning and then applying these in a range of practical examples of techniques and case studies of exemplars of good practice. All the time we wish to move towards the second scenario (Figure 1.1), identifying the aspects which the teachers of tomorrow will have to tackle if they are going to successfully develop learning individuals, in learning teams, in learning organisations for a learning society.

Developments in INSET and professional development

Some ten years ago, INSET and professional development regained centre stage with the publication of Circular 6/86 (DES, 1986) heralding the introduction of the new targeted and earmarked local education authority (LEA) Training Grants scheme which replaced the interim measure of the Technical and Vocational Educational Initiative-Related Inservice Training (TRIST) scheme.

Curiously, the introduction of these initiatives ended a long period in the doldrums for INSET, immediately following the publication of the James

IN-SERVICE TRAINING [1980s]	PROFESSIONAL DEVELOPMENT [1990s]
Fragmented 'ad hoc-racy': rarely co-ordinated within a strategy, funded from many sources, 'pooling', specific grants, education-support grants, LEA funds, etc.	**Professional development plan:** all schools and colleges will have a balanced and co-ordinated strategy for professional development linked to the Development Plan and outcomes from appraisal
Top-down needs identification: by LEA inspectors/advisers, central government, higher education providers, HMI, etc.	**Systematic bottom-up process for needs identification:** which will enable individual teachers to articulate their needs within school, LEA and national priorities
Menu-led INSET courses: leaflets, booklets published and advertised in staff rooms from Higher Education Institutions (HEIs), LEAs, HMI and commercial providers	**Curriculum-led professional development programmes:** tackling both content and process issues, as well as learning and leadership strategies
INSET participants are mainly enthusiastic volunteers: often pursuing personal career development through award bearing courses – BEd, MEd	**All teachers have access to professional development:** enthusiastic volunteers plus other not previously involved identified through needs audits. Confluence of professional development and pupil, school and LEA needs
Little institutional involvement: in identifying types of training needs, individual teachers for training and following up on outcomes of training	**Schools at the centre of the process:** in identifying needs, targeting development priorities, contracting delivery, following up and evaluating outcomes at classroom level
Little individual teacher involvement: in identifying their own needs, deciding how best to meet them within a school framework. Many teachers left out entirely	**Systems ensure involvement of all teachers:** in all stages of the professional development cycle as collaborative learning participants
Little or no systematic evaluation: or concern about the effect of training on the individual teacher or school and none on the ultimate effect on pupils' educational experiences. No attempt to measure the cost-effectiveness of INSET	**Monitoring and evaluation built into the process:** at all levels. Professional development events are evaluated at the point of delivery. Outcomes are evaluated in terms of their effect on pupils, the teacher, schools and the LEA and the lessons fed back into the process. There will be a careful scrutiny of the cost-effectiveness of professional development
INSET regarded as *ipso-facto* a 'good thing' but largely unmanaged, uncoordinated, ad hoc and reactive	**Professional development carefully managed as a rolling programme of staff development within a stated development plan at school, LEA and government levels (as envisaged in DES (1985), ACSET (1984) and Grant-Related In-Service Training (GRIST 1987 on))**

Figure 1.1: Scenarios for professional development in the late twentieth century
(Adapted and updated from Cooper, 1986)

Report (DES, 1972) – perhaps the most forward-looking document on INSET and professional development to come from the Department of Education and Science (DES). Ideas such as a term's sabbatical every seven years for all teachers and the appointment of a professional mentor/INSET co-ordinator in each school were well received at the time but never implemented. This was followed by a very useful document from the Advisory Committee on Induction and Training of Teachers (DES, 1974) which mapped out the principles of a coherent and forward-looking approach to the in-service education and training of teachers. This document identified a framework for the INSET needs of teachers related to the typical stages of their careers:

- **Induction:** first year of teaching, probationary support.
- **Consolidation**: four to six years, adding to professional knowledge and developing skills through short courses.
- **Orientation**: five to eight years, reflection, refreshment, one-term secondment to a centre for advanced studies possibly leading to a change in career direction.
- **Advanced seminars**: eight to 12 years, part-time studies designed to develop specialist expertise in the new career direction and a wider strategic overview of the curriculum.
- **Mid career advanced studies**: 12 to 15 years, where a number of teachers pursue leadership and management training on one-term to one-year secondments as a preparation for middle management.
- **Senior management/refreshment**: a small number of middle managers and administrators preparing for top management and a larger number of long-serving teachers (possibly having spent all their time in one school) getting an opportunity for refreshment, not necessarily on a formal course, to replenish their intellectual and cultural reserves or develop a new interest or enthusiasm for the latter part of their careers.

Having identified these key waypoints in a teacher's career, the Advisory Committee on the Supply and Training of Teachers (ACSTT) (1978) went on to lay out the bones of a process for schools to undertake when managing INSET:

1 Identify the main needs.
2 Decide on and implement the general programme.
3 Evaluate the effectiveness of this general programme.
4 Follow up the ideas gained.

Although these ideas had been described and launched at a time when large-scale audit and examination of the curriculum was taking place as part of the follow-up to James Callaghan's 1976 Ruskin College speech, only a few LEAs and schools took the initiative of implementing them. The overriding concerns at the time were the raising of the school leaving age to 16, a measure which helped stave off impending large-scale youth unemployment for a year or two, and curriculum reform to improve basic skills and examination performance and to relate more specifically to the world of work.

As is often the case, it took a series of targeted and funded initiatives to turn the seminal concepts of the ACSTT into workable practice and everyday experience. This started with the introduction of the TRIST programme.

At the beginning of the TRIST programme, a consensus emerged on the future of professional development in schools which, at the time, was well received and funded. The main points were:

- devolution of funding to schools;
- needs assessment at county and school level;
- school co-ordinators/INSET managers;
- curriculum and pedagogy focused;
- links to appraisal;
- evaluation and accountability for outcomes;
- development planning.

Prior to this initiative, schools had largely relied on a mixture of (relatively) expensive commercial courses, HMI courses such as the Curriculum, Organ-isation, Structure and Management of Schools (COSMOS) weeks and LEA courses provided by advisers. Underlying this was a system of 'pooled' resources for award-bearing courses such as diplomas and masters pro-grammes. Each LEA paid sums of money into a national 'pool'; higher education (HE) institutions ran courses which were recognised for pool funding; individuals applied for places on these courses and for financial support to their LEA. Some LEAs made extensive use of the pool to fund full-time bachelors and masters INSET provision; others were much less generous. In any case there was no clearly planned and coherent provision which took into account all the different needs of teachers at the various stages in their careers.

To some extent this issue of coherence had been addressed in the ACSTT (1978) and Advisory Committee on the Supply and Education of Teachers (ACSET) (1984) reports. Teachers' careers had been mapped out and suggested provision identified. However, it was difficult to impose such a structure on the existing multi-faceted arrangements outlined above. The solution was to use the mechanism developed to fund the Technical and Vocational Initiative (TVEI) to begin to prepare the ground for a more centrally controlled but locally planned system for professional development.

TVEI funding mechanism

The DES had, ever since its inception in the Ministry of Education, been particularly strong on a tradition of protection of what was seen as the finest

7

features of the British education system. Initially this had defended the grammar schools and the independent sector as the main vehicle for identifying a commercial and governmental elite either through birth (and money) or through the development of a meritocracy. Curriculum and learning were largely left to LEAs to sort out, though, in practice, secondary schools developed their own in response to the syllabuses provided by the examination boards for, at first, GCE O and A levels and then for the CSE (which came in as part of the response to the Newsam Report). Primary schools were similarly driven by the need to prepare for the 11+ selection tests.

Three main forces came together to break this cosy relationship between guaranteed funding from the centre through the rate support grant and local LEA/school autonomy over the curriculum: the Ruskin College speech delivered by James Callaghan, Prime Minister in 1976, the Organization for Economic Cooperation and Development (OECD, 1975) report on the British Education System and the 'Yellow Book' from HMI (1976) which addressed the structure of the curriculum. All of these moved the focus to the content and structure of what was being taught in schools and its relationship to the wider socio-economic society.

What was needed, therefore, after a period of investigation and charting of what *was* actually being taught in schools, was a way of addressing the twin issues of updating the content of the curriculum and making it more relevant to the world of work. Since the DES had been particularly ineffective in achieving real change in schools (most of the curriculum initiatives in the 1970s had come from teachers and universities working through agencies such as the Schools Council), a radical mechanism was developed to ensure implementation at the school level of curriculum innovation.

The Initiative was set up, ostensibly, to provide a more work-related curriculum in the upper secondary school and to enable TVEI schools to obtain the latest technology to support this. In governmental terms, it is the way in which this was funded which broke the mould of local/national funding of education. For the reasons outlined above (the traditionalism and establishment nature of the DES) elements of funding were withdrawn from the education parts of the rate support grant, and thus from the control of the DES/LEAs, and redirected through the Department of Employment's training division, the Manpower Services Commission (MSC).

The power of the contract

The MSC had developed considerable expertise and experience in managing government priority directives through its control of the Youth Opportunities and Training Opportunities Programmes (YOPS and TOPS) schemes of job creation in the late 1970s which were designed to soak up youth unemployment.

The TVEI scheme was introduced to make school leavers more employable and the funding was seen at the time to be 'new' money for, in the first instance, much needed equipment.

Although there was much controversy at the time as to why a 'chosen few' schools should receive such generous funding when all schools could do with more money, those LEAs and schools which took part in the first phase were very supportive of the scheme. There was a wide variety of response, varying from one northern LEA which gave all the first-phase money to two schools to a Welsh LEA which managed to ensure all secondary schools gained access to the provision. However, it was the *way* in which the funds were allocated to LEAs and schools which gave the lead to what was to come in terms of earmarked priority funding.

Each LEA was invited to bid for a given amount of funding. These were detailed bids against clearly defined criteria provided by the MSC. The first phase was very competitive (only ten LEAs were successful in that round), the second less so (40 LEAs, roughly a third of those in England and Wales) and the TVEI Extension was available to all remaining secondary schools. LEAs and their schools had to deliver what their bids detailed, develop and carry out monitoring and evaluation procedures and both take ownership of their projects and be accountable for the public funds they had been allocated against the original criteria.

These arrangements amounted to a binding contract between the MSC, as the government's agency, and the LEAs/schools. If the contract was not delivered, funding was withdrawn. In practice, another key mechanism was introduced – a system by which LEAs and schools were given permission to spend against agreed contracts but then had to make quarterly claims in arrears to reclaim the expenditure. It was at this stage that expenditure was disallowed if it was on ineligible items and the schools/LEAs had to cover the expenditure out of their own funds.

This system was carried over to the TRIST initiative (and later the LEA Training Grants Scheme and its successor Grants for Education Support and Training) and has proved to be a powerful mechanism for ensuring compliance with government priorities – so much so that the arrangements for inspection of schools by the Office for Standards in Education (OFSTED) are totally on the basis of bid and contract and the system being set up for delivery of the TTA's framework for professional development also relies on competitive bid and binding contract.

The competence-based training debate

One of the major shifts in training which occurred through the TVEI and TRIST initiatives concerned the move from a menu-led approach of LEA short courses and HEI-led award-bearing (mostly pooled and seconded) programmes to a focus on specific and generic skills-based training.

In the first phase, TVEI had concentrated on plugging the technology gap through the generous provision of equipment. Many schools had purchased sophisticated items such as CAD/CAM lathes, computer-based word processing systems, microwave cookers and food processors but had failed to appreciate the initial resistance to change from teachers who had built up their hard-won manual skills over some considerable period of time, many of them from experience in industry in the days of craft apprenticeships. Such people did not understand how best to use the new equipment and resented expenditure on complex items when basic tools were becoming increasingly expensive and difficult to replace.

By the time the TRIST scheme was introduced (midway through the second phase of TVEI), teachers and LEA advisers had begun to appreciate the need for retraining *before* the introduction of new equipment. External evaluations of TVEI schemes had revealed much of the new technology languishing in store cupboards and consequently, having little impact on the learning experience of pupils. Even those LEAs and schools which had successfully introduced the new technologies began to see the problems of a close concentration on training too specific to a particular piece of equipment or technology as this rapidly dated. Many of us remember the agonies of learning VIEW, EDWORD and other very 'clunky' BBC/CPM-based spreadsheets and word processing suites!

As a result, TRIST training focused on more generic skills, both for teachers and pupils, and the recording of achievement of these through various portfolio and records of achievement approaches. This was designed to enable teachers (and their pupils) to be able to cope with the rapidly changing world of work. It also recognised that education is not just a precursor to life in the real world of work but is part of the socio-economic fabric itself, generating ideas and being a 'child of its time' alongside other aspects of contemporary society. We thus have a parallel and symbiotic relationship between education and the commercial world rather than a linear one.

Parallel to the shift in teacher INSET away from award-bearing courses focusing on intellectual skills towards specific and generic skills-based experience, a debate was taking place on a wider scale in professional development across industry and the professions.

Traditionally, management in the USA and UK had followed different paths of training and development. The US experience typically involved specific management training and dates back to the 1920s and the 'scientific management' school founded by Fred Taylor. The pioneering efforts of Taylorism to reduce shop-floor work functions to time and motion equations and thus remove the human factors which could result, literally, in 'spanners in the works'. Business schools and postgraduate schools of management science taught these principles to managers, so there has been a long tradition of a trained and regularly updated force of managers in the US and a symbiotic relationship between captains of industry and the world of commerce and business.

More recently, in the 1970s, the influence of sociology and psychology was felt in the attempt to diagnose those elements of competency which distinguished the 'best from the rest' – i.e. the attributes of superior managerial performers. This ran alongside the 'excellence' movement characterised by Peters and Waterman's (1982) classic text. Much work was done in this area to identify the generic competencies which underlie such superior performance, one example of which can be seen in the competency list developed by Hay McBer (Everard, 1990) shown in Figure 1.2. These 20 competencies cover 80–90 per cent of the distinguishing characteristics of superior performance in the jobs studied by McBer. The remaining 5 per cent is made up by a competency which differs for different jobs.

By contrast, in the UK there has not been the same tradition of training for managers, either in the business/commercial world or in education, the emphasis being on learning through experience on the shop floor. Consequently the focus has tended to be on job-related specific vocational skills as demonstrated in the courses validated by the Business and Technical

---

ACHIEVEMENT AND ACTION
Achievement orientation
Concern for order
Information seeking
Initiative

HELPING AND HUMAN SERVICE
Interpersonal understanding
Customer service orientation

MANAGERIAL
Developing others
Directiveness
Teamwork and co-operation
Team leadership

COGNITIVE
Analytical thinking
Conceptual thinking
Technical/professional expertise

IMPACT AND INFLUENCE
Influence
Organisational awareness
Relationship building

PERSONAL EFFECTIVENESS
Self-control
Self-confidence
Flexibility
Organisational commitment

Figure 1.2: Hay/McBer competency clusters

Educational Council. Such courses now fall under the umbrella of the National Council for Vocational Qualifications.

Although the Management Charter Initiative (MCI) has developed a three-level scheme for first-line supervisors, middle managers and senior managers, this still focuses on the demonstration of narrow 'can-do' functional skills and competencies. Similarly, the Royal Society of Arts (RSA) middle and senior management standards, validated at National Vocational Qualification (NVQ) levels 4 (first degree-equivalent) and 5 (postgraduate), also require the provision of evidence of managerial performance in a detailed range of vocational tasks. School Management South, a project involving a consortium of 14 LEAs and some 3600 schools, carried out a functional analysis building on the MCI approach to determine the competencies required for educational managers (Earley, 1992). This resulted in the development of a series of key roles (shown in Figure 1.3) with associated units of competence and their elements.

There are, however, a number of more generic frameworks for school managerial competencies which are more closely linked to the approach adopted in the US. Lyons (1976) has developed and validated a framework which has its roots in the work of Saville and Holdsworth (1995) from the field of occupational psychology. The McBer competency clusters have been developed further by the National Association of Secondary School Principals into a set of generic competencies for use in assessment centres to provide information for the selection of candidates for principalship. These have been adapted in turn for the UK context by the National Educational Assessment Centre (NEAC), originally based in Oxford Polytechnic (now Oxford Brookes University) and set up by the Secondary Heads Association with government and industry support (see Figure 1.4).

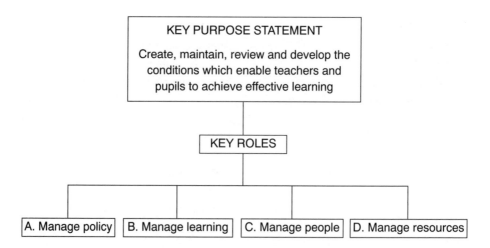

Figure 1.3: School Management South competence framework

ADMINISTRATIVE

1. Problem analysis

2. Judgement

3. Organisational ability

4. Decisiveness

INTERPERSONAL

5. Leadership

6. Sensitivity

7. Stress tolerance

COMMUNICATIVE

8. Oral communication

9. Written communication

PERSONAL BREADTH

10. Range of interest

11. Personal motivation

12. Educational values

Figure 1.4: The NEAC competency framework

The assessment centre approach has been influential on government thinking with the TTA drawing up National Standards for continuing professional development of teachers and educational leaders (TTA, 1997a; 1997b). This approach typically involves an initial review of the candidate's experience and expertise against the competencies, a series of observed and assessed exercises and simulations (such as psychometric tests, in-tray exercises, leaderless groups and presentations) and a one-to-one interview and feedback.

National standards for continuing professional development for teachers

The TTA has been developing a framework for initial training and continuing professional development of teachers to bring coherence into INSET and

13

progression to training and development opportunities. The first stage was the implementation of competencies towards which students undertaking initial teacher training will work. This was followed by the drawing up of a list of tasks and abilities required at the headteacher level. These headteacher competencies are accessible through the Headteacher Leadership and Management Programme (HEADLAMP) for newly appointed heads and the National Professional Qualification for Headship (NPQH) for aspiring heads.

The consultation for the next phase in the TTA's framework for National Professional Standards at key points in the career profile of teachers commenced on 6 December 1996. The standards being developed are for the National Professional Qualification for Subject Leaders (NPQSL). This forms an integral part of the TTA's framework, to which will be added the development of 'Expert Teacher'(replaced by the Advanced Skills Teacher) and Special Educational Needs Co-ordinator (SENCO) standards as well as standards for Newly Qualified Teachers (NQTs) reflecting the 'national curriculum' for initial teacher training.

This will complete the framework, although it is recognised that there are some issues still to be resolved – for example, there is no specific set of standards for those middle managers who have a whole school or pastoral area of responsibility (or indeed anything which is not a 'subject') nor the vital role of deputy head. In time, the HEADLAMP scheme may be phased out as the majority of new heads will have gained the NPQH, in favour of a scheme for medium to long-serving heads wishing to be updated or gain further qualifications.

Although there would seem to be a good case for developing such a framework, there are tensions which are partly revealed in the sets of standards themselves and the order in which they are being developed, just as there was an implicit order of importance in the way in which the subjects of the National Curriculum came on stream – the political agenda is clearly driving this initiative! In summary, then, the framework for teacher professional development through the TTA will be as shown in Figure 1.5.

This brief outline of the development of frameworks and standards for the continuing professional development of teachers highlights some of the tensions and issues in the implementation of a coherent approach to professional learning which mirrors those being developed in the classroom and in the wider economy and at least recognises the need for lifelong learning.

A major problem of all such approaches is the tendency to reductionism resulting from fragmentation of what is, or should be, a holistic set of skills. The key to successful leadership and management lies in the way in which the competencies are combined to solve real-world problems. This means recognising that there are many ways of conceptualising the issues and that the act of conceptualisation will generate a certain set of tasks and skills compatible with and arising from the mind-set which influenced the original conceptualisation.

Stages in the framework	Timescale
• Headteacher Leadership and Management Programme (HEADLAMP) for newly appointed heads.	In place from April 1995.
• National Professional Qualification for Headship (NPQH) for aspiring heads.	Pilot phase 1996–97, fully available from Sept. 1997.
• National Professional Qualification for Subject Leaders (NPQSL) for heads/ co-ordinators of subjects.	Consultation Dec. 1996– Feb. 1997, revised standards issued Autumn 1997, currently 'on hold'.
• 'Expert Teacher' Standards for career class teachers.	On hold pending Advanced Skills Teacher consultation.
• National Professional Qualification for Special Educational Needs Co-ordinators (SENCOs).	Consultation up to Oct. 1997, revised draft 1998.
• National Professional Qualification for Newly Qualified Teachers.	Possibly to follow a reintroduction of the probationary period.
• Development Programme for Serving Heads.	Tender let, being developed 1997/98.

Figure 1.5: The TTA framework for continuing professional development

To illustrate this point we reproduce in Figure 1.6 one framework (Quinn *et al.*, 1996) which attempts to relate a range of eight competencies to four ways of seeing the world and the way it works. This links back to the issue raised above in which the answer to responding successfully to rapid change is in terms of a focus on relationships and processes, rather than structural descriptions, line and branch management systems and narrow job-specific tasks and skills.

Issues in the development of a learning profession

This section explores a range of trends which will have a profound impact on our understanding of what it means to be an effective educationalist in the years to come. The concept of teacher efficacy has remained largely undisturbed for many years. If professional development and learning are to

Outline of TTA national standards for subject leaders and heads

A. National Standards for Headteachers (TTA, 1997a)

The standards are designed to set clear expectations and targets for aspiring headteachers and help to provide a clear focus for them to plan their professional development. Much work in this area has already been undertaken by OFSTED, schools, LEAs, higher education institutions, and other agencies. The standards are derived from that body of work and build on the tasks and abilities in the HEADLAMP scheme. They reflect the considerable work done on management standards by those outside the education profession. The standards for new headteachers will form part of the TTA's wider work on developing national standards for five key points in the profession: newly qualified teachers; expert/advanced skills teachers; SENCOs; experts in subject leadership and management; and experts in school leadership and management.

The draft standards for the national professional qualification for headship are in four parts:

1 **Core purpose of headship:** to provide professional leadership for a school which secures its success and improvement, ensuring high quality education for all its pupils and improved standards of achievement.

2 **Key outcomes of headship:** ethos, teaching, pupil progress, parent partnership, governors' responsibilities, efficient/effective use of resources.

3 **Professional knowledge and understanding:** quality, data handling including ICT, curriculum, assessment and teaching, leadership and management, political/legal framework, governance.

4 **Skills and attributes:** leadership, decision making, communication, self-management.

5 **Key area of headship:**
    (a) strategic direction and development of the school;
    (b) teaching and learning;
    (c) leading and managing staff;
    (d) efficient and effective deployment of staff;
    (e) accountability.

B. Consultation on a National Professional Qualification for Subject Leaders (TTA, 1997b)

The key target group for this qualification is heads of subjects at secondary level and subject co-ordinators at primary level. The NPQSL will be based on national standards for subject leaders . . . [which] . . . should set clear and explicit expectations of subject leaders enabling them, and schools, to set targets for professional development and career progression. Much of the work in this area has already been undertaken by subject associations, OFSTED, LEAs, higher education institutions and other agencies both within and outside education. The revised standards, developed in consultation with teachers, headteachers, people from higher education and the wider community, reflect this work and are based on current good practice in the field.

The national standards provide a focus for the training, development and assessment of subject leaders. They define the core purpose, key outcomes, knowledge, understanding, skills and abilities required to perform effectively and provide a focus for training, development and assessment by identifying key tasks to be performed by subject leaders.

The revised national standards for subject leaders are in five parts:

1 **Core purpose of subject leadership:** To provide professional leadership for a subject to secure high quality teaching and effective use of resources and ensure improved standards of achievement for all pupils.

2 **Key outcomes of subject leadership:** pupil progress, teacher effectiveness, parent support, knowledgeable subject leaders, liaison with support staff and community.

3 **Professional knowledge and understanding:** curriculum and pedagogy, current research, data handling including information and communications technology (ICT), literacy, numeracy, spiritual, moral, social, cultural, mental and physical development, governance, special educational needs (SEN), health and safety.

4 **Skills and attributes:** leadership, decision-making communication, self-management.

5 **Key areas of subject leadership:**
   (a) teaching, learning and the curriculum;
   (b) monitoring, evaluating and improving;
   (c) people and relationships;
   (d) managing resources;
   (e) accountability.

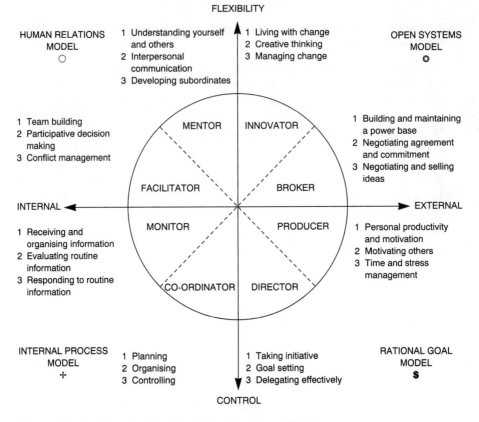

Figure 1.6: A coherent and relativistic competency model
(*Source:* Quinn *et al.*, 1996, p. 16. © 1996 John Wiley & Sons Inc; reprinted by permission of John Wiley & Sons Inc.)

be seen as valid, relevant and appropriate then they need to both cater for current needs and demands and anticipate changes to help schools move from reaction and crisis implementation to anticipation and prevention. The major cause of short-term responses is, of course, the nature of educational policy making at a national, political level. Policy making for education has not been a coherent process based on any notion of successful implementation. Hague (1997) explains this as follows:

> *Despite – perhaps because of – the fact that politicians understand education so little, they too often engage in what David Hargreaves, in an outspoken critique, calls 'utopian social engineering'. An ideal is defined – comprehensive education or the National Curriculum for example – and very large sums of money are found with no apparent difficulty to spend on this ideal. Yet, instead of being subject to local trials in a number of schools and disseminated . . . these utopian policies are generated with enormous confidence and then subjected to instant implementation. (p. 124)*

What is most disturbing about this analysis is that the policy-making process bears no relationship to any model of learning or development. There is a profound schism between those who make policy and those who have to implement it in LEAs, schools and classrooms.

A central thesis of this book is that there has to be a high correlation between what has to be done and how it is done. Planning, policy making and organisational and staff development have to be macrocosms of the core purpose of education – children's learning. If they are not, or at least trying to be, then there are dangers of moral inconsistency, incrementalism and partial implementation. Many of the problems that exist with policy making, school organisations and the development and deployment of teaching staff stem from the lack of shared understanding of how children learn. The relationship between these elements is fundamental to the discussion in this section.

Gardner (1997, pp. 109–10) argues that much of the thinking about education is compromised by three biases which he characterises as 'Westist', 'Testist' and 'Bestist'. 'Westist' refers to the Western intellectual tradition which places a high value on logical thinking and rationality to the exclusion of other qualities. 'Testist' describes the emphasis on those 'human abilities and approaches which are readily testable, (p. 109). Assessment is too restrictive and often inhumane. 'Bestist' refers to the supremacy of one certain approach – usually logical – the mathematical. Much of the thinking about education is compromised by these biases which might explain why it often functions in a deficit mode usually resonant of the nineteenth century.

In the context of professional learning evidence for this can be found in the vocabulary of training and courses, the emphasis on competencies and the confidence that inspection, assessment and observation can actually produce valid and reliable information. The context in which schools are increasingly having to function challenges the integrity of these approaches.

Megatrends

Any attempt at futurology will always be compromised by uncertainty and the impossibility of prediction with confidence. The relationship between prophecy and planning is an uncertain one. However, it is possible to identify a number of trends that are currently significant, and extrapolate them to draw tentative conclusions.

In social terms it is possible to identify a number of fundamental changes taking place:

- The population is ageing with an ever increasing proportion living, and remaining healthy, for more years than ever before.

- The proportions of one-parent families, people remaining unmarried and people living on their own are all increasing.
- There is evidence of ethnic groups becoming more insular in order to protect the integrity of their cultural values.
- The proportion of people living in endemic poverty is increasing and remains stubbornly resistant to social policies.

Economic trends that will have a potential impact on the nature of education include:

- the size of the workforce diminishing with a smaller percentage earning a disproportionate amount of the salaries available;
- changes in the patterns of working with more home-based, part-time jobs;
- increasing numbers of low-paid, low-skill jobs in the service sector;
- greater globalisation with companies functioning under international rather than national laws, e.g. in regard to the location of work in low-pay economies;
- the emergence of areas of habitual high unemployment and social distress;
- the increasing inability of social institutions, e.g. health care and social services, to respond to need.

The third element is information technology which continues to grow at an exponential rate. Its impact on work, leisure, education and all aspects of ordinary social life continues to develop in rapid and often unpredictable ways. What is clear is that:

- more information is available to more people than ever before;
- fundamental changes are taking place both in how work is done and in the nature of work;
- communication, in all its forms, is becoming faster, cheaper and more accurate.

The impact of these three trends might appear to be one inducing profound pessimism. Indeed it could be argued that optimism about the future is restricted to those who form the social, economic and educational elite. Schools are only one factor in a complex social equation yet they cannot remain the same if they are to remain true to their perceived social function. But this will require them to undergo a fundamental reorientation. As Drucker (1993) puts it:

> That the school will now increasingly be in society may therefore be as radical a change as any in teaching and learning methods, in subject matter, or in the teaching and learning process. Schools will continue to teach the young ... Schools will have to become organised for lifelong learning. Schools will have to become 'open systems'. (p. 204)

The implications of this view for the conceptualisation of the role of the teacher, and the related implications for the education, development and learning of teachers, are fundamental and profound. If learning in schools is to change then a fundamental starting point is not so much what teachers learn as how they learn.

Achievement and accountability

Changing interpretations of economic performance and the perceived high correlation between economic success and educational achievement have meant an increased emphasis on school and individual performance. This has emerged at the same time as an increased emphasis on organisational and individual accountability, the manifestations of which in England and Wales include: OFSTED inspections, publication of raw-data league tables and changing relationships with governing bodies.

There are numerous conceptual and practical problems with the related imperatives of achievement and accountability – not the least of which is the issue of how both are to be defined. Most of the language employed around these issues is historic:

> The underlying task for the future, however, is not only to deal with the really disastrous schools, but also the comfortable schools that on the surface appear effective or at least satisfactory and enjoy public support, but which in reality are mediocre: 'the good schools – if this were 1965'. (Stoll and Fink, 1996, p. 2)

A twofold response is required. Schools are legally obliged to work towards demonstrating achievement and accountability in '1965' terms. At the same time there is a moral and professional imperative to begin to look to new measures of performance and demonstrate accountability to new stakeholders. Current measures are inappropriate in that they measure the wrong things in the wrong way, they are *post facto* and, most importantly, are not designed on the basis of organisational learning for improvement. Darling-Hammond (1997) argues that *genuine* accountability

> ... is achieved when a school system's policies and operating practices work both to provide good education and to correct problems as they occur. An effective accountability system is designed to increase the likelihood of successful practices, ferret out harmful practices, and provide internal self-corrections – feedbacks, assessments and incentives – that support continual improvement. (p. 245)

For Darling-Hammond it is an essential prerequisite of any model of accountability that teachers have the 'knowledge and skills to teach effectively' (*ibid*.). While the demands of public accountability will always be constrained by political factors it is possible for schools to develop their own models based on:

● definitions of appropriate standards;

- policies to ensure consistent application of those standards;
- strategies to ensure the capacity of individuals to understand and apply the standards;
- development strategies to reinforce and improve the standards;
- personal and institutional self-review to ensure accurate data to inform improvement strategies.

Professional learning and development is the central factor in enhancing both achievement and accountability. It is impossible to raise pupil achievement without raising teacher achievement, and professional accountability has to include a commitment to improvement through professional learning. The biggest conceptual shift in the context of raising achievement and increasing accountability is to see them focused on preventing failure rather than reacting to it. Central to this is an understanding of learning.

Learning

Chapter 3 discusses this issue in greater depth than is appropriate here. The issue for the design of professional learning and development is the extent to which it serves as an exemplar for, is congruent with and a model for learning for everyone in the school community.

Few concepts are as elusive in the everyday discourse of schools as what actually constitutes learning. For many learning is either the result of teaching or the capacity to demonstrate acquired knowledge and skills. Without a sophisticated understanding of the nature of learning there is the danger that teaching will be seen as the necessary and sufficient requirement for it to take place rather than a fundamentally significant variable. The interaction between how teachers teach and how they learn is complex but it is worth speculating that models of professional learning are an important determinant of teacher behaviour (rather like the probably apocryphal one-hour lecture on how lectures cease to be effective after 20 minutes).

There is a very strong case for arguing that the dichotomy between children's learning and that of adults is an arbitrary and artificial one. What schools need are policies and strategies for learning which are fundamental to every aspect of the school's functioning. The issues surrounding the problem of defining learning are explored in depth by Bowring-Carr and West-Burnham (1997). The key principles informing any discussion of the nature of learning can be summarised as:

- learning is an individual and subjective process;
- there are numerous outcomes to any learning activity and these will be significantly determined by the mode of assessment;

- learning is the result of the interaction of a range of variables, most of which are personal rather than generic and teaching is only one of these variables;
- replication and memorisation are indicators of shallow, transient learning – profound learning is exemplified by personal understanding;
- learning is a product of neurological and sociological factors;
- learning is not linear.

It may be worth reflecting on the extent to which there are parallels between the management of a classroom and the management of an in-service course and how far both take the principles of learning outlined above into account. It is not overstating the case to assert that pupil learning, and so achievement, is a direct correlation of teacher learning, that the relationship between the two is symbiotic and that the behaviour of teachers, managers and leaders is the most powerful exemplification of the relationship.

Leadership

There is an overwhelming consensus that school improvement is a direct function of leadership. Almost every model of improvement, effectiveness, change and quality has at its heart the existence of leadership. In their study *Success Against the Odds* the National Commission for Education (1996) found that leadership was a crucial determinant of a school's success:

> *In schools serving disadvantaged and frequently troubled areas, an abundance of energy and commitment is needed just to tread water ... A headteacher, more than anyone else, has the capacity to bring about such a release of energy and, even more importantly, a belief in the school's potential to succeed. (pp. 335–6)*

If leadership is fundamental to school improvement and success then it is not unreasonable to speculate that it might also be a crucial factor in teams, classrooms and every social unit of the school. One of the most significant barriers to school improvement has been the focus on leadership as a hier-archical function characteristically located at the 'top' of the organisational pyramid with everyone else in a dependent mode. This can be partly attributed to cultural norms which see leadership as an organisational role rather than a personal characteristic. It is also a function of the formal, bureaucratic model of individual accountability which pervades headship in England and Wales. If there is to be whole-school improvement then it can be argued that leadership has to be pervasive and that it has to be seen as a natural component of every individual's functioning.

If this proposition is accepted then it follows that a key outcome of professional learning is the enhancement of leadership capacity and potential for all. There are numerous models available of the components of leadership but they can probably be reduced to a number of simple maxims:

1 The existence of a vision of how things should be coupled with a moral sense of how to get there.

2 An awareness of the importance of human relationships and the need for respect, recognition, reinforcement and communication.

3 The capacity to get things done, to make things happen and to deliver outcomes which are consistent with the vision and moral purpose.

Even at this simplified level there is nothing in this list that is not appropriate to the school, team and classroom. The issue is not so much the scale or significance of what has to be done as the way in which it is done. Improvement and development are never managed, they have to be led.

This is not to diminish the significance of management and administration – both are essential but they have to be contextualised by leadership. In essence leadership is much more than management omnicompetence – the curriculum (as a body of knowledge and skills) can be managed but learning requires leadership.

The implications of this proposition for professional learning and development are profound. Although knowledge acquisition and skills development are vital they are only valid in the context of the enhancement of an individual's leadership capability. Leadership, in this context, is not the accumulation of the components of a competency profile but rather the engagement in a process which is quintessentially concerned with learning in that it is personal, creates understanding and so provides the capacity to act. It may be more appropriate to view leadership as a capacity to learn rather than the partial attainment of a set of discrete characteristics. The primary criterion for leadership is the ability to learn from experiences in order to enhance the capability to deploy qualities. If leadership is to be developed in everyone then they have to be helped to process their personal and professional experiences through a value system and in response to others in order to evolve a growing understanding of what it means to be a leader.

Sergiovanni (1996) provides a powerful model integrating leadership and learning

> *Teachers practise a form of pedagogical leadership directly since in schools they stand first and closest in a caring relationship to children . . . the process of education itself implies leadership. (p. 93)*

> *Mobilising the school community on behalf of problem solving is practising leadership as a form of pedagogy.*

> *When principals practise leadership as pedagogy, they exercise their stewardship responsibilities by committing themselves to building, to serving, to caring for, and to protecting the school and its purposes. (p. 95)*

An important hypothesis (that will have to remain untested for the time being) is that the most effective practitioners of pedagogical leadership (teachers or headteachers) are those who are the most effective learners. Sergiovanni's list of qualities points to a capacity to understand – the pivotal determinant of learning.

A further factor worthy of consideration at this stage is that the principles of leadership learning can also be applied to the education of pupils. While they need skills to manage their learning they also need to be able to develop the leadership qualities that will enhance their capacity to work in a collaborative way and to reconcile personal learning with the need to recognise and respect the needs of others.

Individual and organisational learning

The perceived tension between individual and organisational needs is one of the abiding problems in managing professional learning. On the one hand is the fact that learning is an individual phenomenon and subject to personal motivations and priorities. Against this are the needs of the organisation which, it is argued, has superordinate priorities and, in the final analysis, controls resources. Reconciling this tension is seen as one of the most delicate balancing acts in school management. It has to be recognised that individual commitment is vital if any programme of professional development is to work and that the legitimate aspiration to career development is a fundamental right. It also has to be acknowledged that schools have to function as organisations.

Historically this paradox has usually been reconciled in favour of organisational imperatives. This has led to generic training, a high degree of instrumentality and a reductionist approach to what constitutes developmental activities. The diametrically opposed view is that any form of developmental activity is valid if it involves the teacher in learning and that specific skills and knowledge are less significant than the process of understanding what it is to be a learner.

The tension can be seen as profoundly artificial in that it postulates a false dichotomy between work and training. It also implies an astonishingly high degree of confidence on the part of the organisation that it has a monopoly of truth as to the developmental needs, learning styles, current state of skills and knowledge of every individual as well as detailed understanding of what the organisation's needs really are.

The crucial issue in this context is not so much a detailed schedule of organisational needs as the coherent and systematic articulation of the school's values and policies and then facilitation for each individual to help them achieve them. This issue is explored in greater depth in Chapter 2 – the notion of the learning organisation creates a model which integrates individual and organisational learning.

One outstanding issue in this context is the whole question of career development. For most teachers career development is perceived as a struggle to ascend the hierarchy – the notion of a vertical career. Horizontal career development – becoming expert at a particular type of job – is less common as a strategy because of the inescapable link between status and salary. The reluctance to support developmental activities which are explicitly personal and linked to promotion prospects is understandable in terms of prioritising scarce resources but is fallacious. It is in the process of studying that most learning takes place; the award of a higher degree or completion of a long programme of study is arbitrary as a measure of impact on performance. Indeed it may well be most beneficial for a school to 'lose' a teacher after such a programme. It is much more advantageous to have staff who are in the process of learning than those who have 'completed' their studies.

A further issue is that in a professional, team-based culture every effort should be made to develop 'home-grown' talent. As schools develop 'flatter' structures the notion of incremental progression up the ladder will diminish in significance, most notably in secondary schools. Vertical career development, while still significant, will become less important than updating, developing flexibility and learning to work in new ways to meet new demands.

Conclusion

This chapter has sought to place the short- and long-term issues facing the management of professional development and learning in context. Although the imperatives of government policy, OFSTED, etc. are direct and compelling there is also a need to be aware of future thinking, in particular of what Caldwell (1997) refers to as the 'Virtual School'. The combined effects of information technology, changing patterns of employment and a fundamental redefinition of the nature and purpose of education require learning and development strategies concerned with profound strategic change as well as tactical responses.

Two trends in particular will possibly compel a profound re-education of teachers, managers and leaders in schools. First is the increasing understanding of how we learn, in particular the work of Gardner and others focusing on neurological functioning and the physiology as well as the psychology of cognitive development. Secondly, the changing status of knowledge and methods of learning brought about by information technology will have a profound and fundamental effect on the role of teachers and the nature of schools as organisations. The management of professional learning has to be functional but it also needs to be humane to help individuals prepare for fundamental changes that will challenge many of the cultural norms on which their working lives have been postulated.

In summary, any school developing a policy for professional development and learning will need to address the following key issues:

- megatrends, riding the waves of history, strategic intent, empowerment for all;
- individual autonomy vs school/section priorities;
- career patterns, portfolio occupations;
- leadership, managerialism, administration and learning;
- process, product, procedures, people;
- adding value to the learning process at all stages.

2
■ ■ ■

The Learning Organisation – Reengineering Schools for Lifelong Learning

Introduction

It has taken some two decades for the concept of the learning organisation to achieve recognition as a powerful way of reengineering for lifelong learning. During this time, schools have been through a period of very rapid change but, paradoxically, many look less like learning organisations today than they may have before the introduction of the Education Reform Act 1988. This chapter examines some of the key ideas behind the learning organisation, explores why the concept is so powerful in contemporary contexts, identifies various types of learning organisations and suggests an analytical technique for relating styles of organisational learning to the environmental context. The chapter concludes with an analysis of the implications of learning organisation concepts for schools and school leaders.

The learning organisation – the context

'The one constant factor in contemporary society is the exponential increase in the rate of change' (anon.) – so, tomorrow will be different to what we expect and before we get used to this, it will change anyway! To respond successfully to rapidly changing environments and markets, organisations need to learn at least as quickly as the prevailing rate of change – otherwise they are forever playing catch-up.

Over the past decade or so a great deal of experience has been developed as regards what works in such contexts. For instance, 'lean and fit' companies, it is argued, respond more rapidly, give greater customer satisfaction and are more likely to prosper. However, the perception held by individuals in such organisations (or, possibly, those recently 'let go' from them) may well be that they see such rapid change as creating intolerable levels of stress – the game is no longer the one they thought they were playing and their sense of being in tune with their world is disrupted, so they become dysfunctional and unable to operate effectively in their organisation. Sociologists would categorise this as being in a state of anomie or normlessness; psychologists might interpret it as a disruption of the individual's 'mind-set' and, possibly, a type of learning disability. In contrast, others who thrive on the constantly reforming challenges characteristic of the *fin de siècle* period can become 'change junkies', unable to settle down to any form of routine and relying on their professional or business instincts to keep them ahead of what they see as the opposition.

There are, however, alternative arguments refuting this notion of the ever-increasing rapidity of change. Since recorded history, writers have lamented on the frivolity and restlessness of, particularly, the young and have harkened back to a 'golden age' when things were more stable, values more clearly lived by and society more ordered and supportive of individuals and their loved ones. With the 20/20 vision of hindsight, we can see that some of the eras during which such opinions were stated were actually 'cusp points' in the evolving chaos of history after which relative stability returned, rather than points on an exponentially rising curve of change. It may well be that we are, at present, near such a cusp point – the collapse of the communist Eastern bloc in favour of Western-style free-market economies is one possible indicator of this – but looking back from 100 years into the next millennium things might look very different.

Nevertheless, there is still a sense in which we can identify a number of powerful 'megatrends' which appear to lie within the unfolding vista of history as clear pointers to a future which will be very different from today. Naisbitt and Aburdene (1990) identified a range of trends which seemed to them to catch the tide of history, and since their seminal text there has grown up a global cottage industry in predicting such megatrends (see, for example, the TAIPAN UK organisation, 1995). While identifying megatrends is an interesting and useful device for enhancing thinking and scenario planning about the range of possibilities which might form the context in which we will work in the days and years to come, it does not, in itself, ensure that we will possess the techniques and understanding for actually living, surviving and succeeding in an unknowable future. What needs to happen, therefore, is a better societal and individual understanding of the relationship between the change process, styles of learning, organisational development and the ongoing life cycles and paradigms of both contemporary culture and unfolding history.

Given a list of social and economic trends such as that presented in Figure 2.1, it is certain that individuals' (and organisations') ultimate success depends on

Social megatrends	Economic megatrends
• Decline of the nuclear family	• Increasing quality and quantity
• Changing age profile	• Globalisation of communication
• Increasing cultural distinctiveness – multiculturalism	• Capacity/cost ratios changing exponentially (things get cheaper, quicker)
• Decline of the Welfare State and other individual and family support	• Replacing symbolic knowledge and the organisations which provide them (established wisdom challenged)
• Emergence of an underclass – the 'have nots' – in all countries	• Access to anything, anywhere by anybody
• Changing gender roles	• The rise of 'information crime' – hacking, viruses, plagiarism, 'chip piracy'
• Rise of the global competitive market	• Growth of the 'information black market'
• Transnational companies – contrasted with increasing autonomy and flatter organisational structures at the work unit level	• Integrated media – tele- and video-conferencing, interactive video and TV, tele-shopping

Figure 2.1: Social and economic megatrends
(*Source:* Jones and O'Sullivan, 1997)

their ability to learn at least as fast as the prevailing rate of change. Those who are more successful will be characterised by their skill in learning faster than the rate of change and in their ability to buck the trend of history by getting, and staying, ahead of the game. The following sections outline some of the key concepts in realigning learning for an uncertain future.

Educational and management megatrends

The skill of being able to identify a key trend in the tide of history *as it develops* is patently demonstrated in the output of the 'gurus' of organisational and development thinking. Such worthies have been able to encapsulate complex analyses and concepts into simple, readily understood models. Examples are Peters and Waterman (1982) – excellence, Hammer and Champy (1993) – reengineering, Morgan (1986) – creative organisational thinking, Deming (1983) and Juran (1979) – quality, Bennis and Nanus (1985) – leadership, Belbin (1981) – teams, Mintzberg (1994) – strategic planning, not forgetting Handy (1994) – most things! Each of these has taken an aspect of organisational behaviour and constructed an elegant framework around it which has fundamentally changed the way we view organisational development.

We are not free of such an approach in education with such notables as Fullan (1982 – change), Caldwell and Spinks (1988 – restructuring/site-based management), Hargreaves (1991 – development planning), Hopkins (1994 – school improvement), Reynolds (1992 – school effectiveness), not to mention the influence of Woodhead (OFSTED), Tate (Schools Curriculum and Assessment Authority – (SCAA)) and Millet (TTA). National curriculum, assessment, appraisal, local self-management, pupil standards, raising achievement, baseline assessment, teachers' National Standards (NQT, NPQSL, NPQH, HEADLAMP and Expert Classroom Teacher – TTA, 1996) all form aspects of the 'new model army' of teaching in Britain.

So what is the highest common factor which might bring together such developments for teachers, pupils and their communities? Returning to the notion of success hinging on the ability to learn in times of rapid change, commercial concerns have seized upon the concept of the learning organisation as one response to the need for rapid organisational development. Ironically, just as the focus changes in industry away from narrow issues of control to the wider field of learning, in education it has swung in the reverse direction – towards control (inspection), teaching (professional standards), bureaucracy/ efficiency (Local Management of Schools (LMS)/Grant Maintained Schools (GMS) and testing (National Curriculum (NC)). Yet again we are facing the prospect of the pendulum swinging one way in the world outside education and the opposite way within the system. Now is the time to wrest learning back for the profession – particularly headteachers and their senior and middle management – in other words: to reinvent schools as truly learning organis- ations and reengineer their structures and processes for lifelong learning.

Approaches to modelling learning

The idea of organisational learning has evolved over at least half a century stemming from the work of Lewin (1946) on experiential learning. However, learning theory itself, of course, goes back a great deal further than this – though, strangely, the philosophical, psychological, sociological and organisational strands have tended to remain somewhat discrete. To illustrate this, the philosophical and psychological models of learning could be represented as in Figure 2.2.

As in the above example, sociological notions of learning reflect the various paradigms in the parent social sciences, from the functional-structuralist perspective which views learning as a socialisation process where individuals are inculcated with the prevailing societal norms of behaviour and ways of thinking, through the symbolic interactionist view that thinking and learning arise from mental debates between the self and significant/generalised others, to phenomenological stances which seek to uncover the hidden rules of behaviour through 'bracketing the world outside', i.e. suspending belief in the world in order to expose the hidden rules of behaviour. In each case, learning is essentially a social activity, often counter-illustrated by tales of feral children who have been unable to learn because of their separation from society.

It has been argued that organisations as such do not (or, indeed, cannot) learn – it is the individuals inside the organisation who do the learning. Much as in the 'nature/nurture' debate, whether this is so is rather academic. If learning is seen as a social activity, then the individual will experience learning as part of a group and thus the organisation can also be conceived of as a learning organisation. If learning is seen as a social activity, and organisations are the location for most of us most of the time, then all organisations must be learning in some way all of the time. It may well be that the learning is inappropriate, dysfunctional or deviant but, nevertheless, it is taking place. One of the benefits of changes with which teachers have had to cope in the past two decades has been a more eclectic and situational approach to teaching and learning styles –

PHILOSOPHY	PSYCHOLOGY
• Neoclassical/ humanist	• Behaviourist
• Vocational	• Cognitive
• Liberal-meritocratic	• Problem-solving
• Liberal progressive	• Gestalt
• Socially critical	• Experiential
• Religious	• Developmental
• Pragmatic	• Meta-cognition
	• Work-based

Figure 2.2: Models of learning

making the activity suit the context and participants. Such a refocusing on learning as a response to rapid change means the teaching profession needs to figure much more prominently in the regeneration of society.

Characteristics of the learning organisation

In the organisational learning field, there are two main strands – the 'learning styles' approach which is rooted in the psychology of management development (Honey and Mumford, 1986), used as both a diagnostic and development tool, and the 'learning organisation' approach (Senge, 1990) which stems from systems thinking. In the former case, Mumford, building on the work of Kolb (1984) and Lewin (1946) on the concept of the learning cycle, developed a typology of four learning styles (activist, reflector, theorist, pragmatist), each of which represents a point on a cycle of learning approaches. Honey and Mumford maintain that each of us has a preference for working in one of these modes more than the others. Knowing your preferred learning style allows you to determine how best you learn individually but it also identifies other possible styles which you need to develop more fully so that you can support others in their own learning through a knowledge of *their* preferred learning styles.

There is evidence that professions and vocations have group preferences and the learning styles inventory lists norms for a number of these. Within a particular professional group there can be a shift in overall preference for a certain learning style in response to changing environmental contexts over time (Kelly, 1995).

This acceptance of the power of individual and group learning in the development of effective organisations is also shown in the growing number of courses and management development texts which are based at least partly on a model for self-development (Hall *et al.*, 1996, Quinn *et al.*, 1996, Whetten *et al.*, 1994). A focus on learning at the individual level and at the group level through team building, for example, is not, however, a sufficient condition for characterising the whole organisation as a learning organisation.

From work that has been done over the past two decades, various writers (particularly Pedler, Burgoyne and Boydell, 1987) have summarised what the range of conditions for learning organisations are and perhaps the simplest and most applicable summary of these is provided by Garratt (1990, pp. 78–9):

1. *A perception of learning as a cyclical process.*
2. *An acceptance of the different roles of policy, strategy and operations within the organisation.*
3. *A free flow of authentic information.*
4. *The ability to value people as the key asset for organisational learning.*

5. *The ability to reframe information at the strategic level: first and second order change.*

Having established what the key conditions are, Holly (1994) moves beyond categorising the key features and identifies, from a number of sources in the field, what learning organisations actually *do*. This is potentially a more powerful way of looking at the concept as it brings together both the types of action that need to be undertaken and illustrates the range of approaches as follows (pp. 132–6):

- *Learning Organisations look to the future by looking at their present.*
- *Learning Organisations institutionalise reflection-in-action.*
- *Learning Organisations treat planning [and evaluation] as learning.*
- *Learning Organisations pace their learning and their development.*
- *Learning Organisations attend to the new 'disciplines'.*
- *Learning Organisations learn from themselves.*
- *Learning Organisations are life-long learners.*

to both of these lists I would add that

- Learning organisations use meta-learning, that is they learn how to learn.

In the USA work on learning organisations arose from systems thinking, which itself originates from an engineering/technology background. Although there is a tendency for such approaches to resemble wiring diagrams and plumbing schematics, at least this is attempting to recognise organisational development (and learning) as an ongoing process rather than just a list of attributes and, as such, avoids the worst effects of reductionism through fragmentation. This systemic approach is typified by Senge's (1990) model of the five disciplines of a learning organisation: personal mastery, shared vision, mental models, team learning and, the 'fifth discipline', systems thinking. The implication is that a truly 'learning organisation' needs to possess all of these to a high degree.

However, in all of these conceptualisations of the learning organisation, there is still the implication that there is only one sort of learning organisation and you are either there because these characteristics typify your organisation or you are 'working towards' being a learning organisation. More recently, having established a wide range of learning style norms from working in management development over many years, Mumford (1994) is beginning to consider whether groups and whole organisations have identifiable learning styles which relate to those of the preferred learning styles of individuals. Indeed, just as managers and leaders need to work through all these management styles in response to their changing environment, organisations may move through the cycle, using different styles depending upon the stage of development at the time or position in the organisational life cycle – of which more below. We thus have the possibility of at least four types of learning organisations, paralleling the four individual learning styles.

Swieringa and Wierdsma (1992), in their formulation, also identify four types of learning organisations: entrepreneurial, prescriptive, unlearning and learning. In each case they describe a different approach to learning as being the distinguishing feature which determines the category into which the organisation fits best. This recognises that all organisations learn; just as all individuals learn; the issue is how effective is their learning and how closely does it match the stage in the cycle of development and the needs of the change context in which the organisation finds itself?

The organisational life cycle

The concept of life cycle is an interesting one in this context. It has been most thoroughly developed, perhaps, in the field of strategic planning and marketing (Johnson and Scholes, 1993) where it is used both to characterise the stage of development of the whole organisation (typically: embryonic, growth, maturity, decline) and also in analysing the balance of the product range in order to ensure new products are being developed and mature products maintained or possibly phased out. Applied to learning organisation thinking it gives another dimension to the type of learning that might be appropriate at each stage in the life cycle.

The life cycle concept is developed further in the marketing field where types (and amounts) of customers are categorised depending on which particular stage in the product life cycle they identify with (innovators 2.5 per cent, early adopters 13.5 per cent, early majority 34 per cent, late majority 34 per cent, laggards 16 per cent). The model is then used to review the company's spread of products to ensure they are designed to appeal to particular segments of the market.

If we take the style of learning (for argument's sake I have chosen the psychological set of models given above) as one axis and the life-cycle stage as the other we can develop a framework onto which we can plot the organisation under review as shown in Figure 2.3.

This is, however, only the first stage of the analysis. In order to develop a tool for judging the appropriateness of the learning style to the stage of development of the organisation, we have to consider issues of 'fit' and 'congruence' (Lawler, 1992). These concepts have been developed through an examination of strategies which are used in organisations to achieve competitive advantage. Although largely arising from the business context, his ideas have powerful implications for schools and colleges in the new education marketplace.

Lawler's characterisation of the high involvement organisation describes not only *how* the different elements combine to create a high involvement

LIFE CYCLE STAGE / STYLE OF LEARNING	Embryonic	Growth	Shakeout	Maturity	Decline
Behaviourist					
Cognitive					
Developmental					
Gestalt					
Experiential					
Problem-solving					
Work-based					
Meta-cognition					

Figure 2.3: Organisational learning styles and the life cycle – a framework for analysis

organisation but also *why* such a formulation brings success in the marketplace. He considers the relationship between elements of the organisation as functions in an equation – this can be simplified as the 'multiplier' effect. Briefly, this means that the elements and aspects which align act as multipliers in the whole equation rather than just being summed. The effect of this is to show that if any one element or aspect is zero then the whole equation resolves as zero. Lawler is focusing on high involvement management in flat organisational structures and the equation works out thus:

$$\text{Involvement} = \text{Information} \times \text{Knowledge} \times \text{Power} \times \text{Rewards}$$

However, the quantum leap in thinking is in his account of *how* the various elements of management combine together and relate to these sources of competitive advantage. The multiplier effect is one of these concepts; the others are those of *fit* and *congruence*. As Lawler puts it: '... no one part of an organisation can be evaluated without knowing its role in the whole system' (1992, p. 52). Following Leavitt (1965) and a long line of subsequent writers who identify from three to seven or more core elements which need to fit together if the system is to perform effectively, Lawler expresses a preference for four:

- **People:** intrinsic motivation, social cohesion, self-managing.

- **Task/technology:** type of production – process, sequential, custom.
- **Information processes:** free interchange – downwards and upwards.
- **Structure:** vertical, horizontal, 'front end – back end', network.

The notion of congruence progresses beyond the appreciation of which particular aspects of an organisation are the ones to 'get right', to an understanding of *how* the parts interact: 'Congruence exists when individuals at all levels in an organisation are rewarded based upon how effectively they exercise the power that is associated with their position and they have the information and knowledge to exercise their power effectively' (1992, p. 57). Unlike many other writers, however, Lawler does not prescribe one 'ideal' set of these relationships but recognises that in some contexts a hierarchical top-down approach is appropriate whereas in others a bottom-up or high involvement approach is more effective. His point is that the aspects or parts of the organisation that need to fit together are the same in any management approach as are the elements of congruence, and it is these that need to be 'aligned' or have a coherent relationship with each other.

Although Lawler is advocating flatter management structures and therefore more involvement in management activities by a wider range of the workforce (high involvement management) he does recognise that other management structures may be more appropriate in other contexts – the important thing is that the elements and aspects of management need to align effectively to gain maximum synergy in the organisation.

So we have the beginnings of a framework which can be used to look at the type of learning going on in organisations and relate this to models of learning and stages in the life cycle of the organisation. We also have a powerful mechanism for looking at the way in which elements of learning might fit together to enhance synergy and also, incidentally, a way of linking personal growth to team and organisational learning. The task is now to test the framework empirically and begin to determine when a reengineering approach might be required as against that of incremental adjustment.

Reengineering for lifelong learning

Having established that there are many different types of learning organis-ations there remains the question as to whether what has been traditionally described as a learning organisation (see Garratt and Holly above) is the pinnacle of an hierarchical list or whether the various types of learning organisations fit best with a particular stage in the organisational life cycle, i.e. is a hierarchical or situationally relative view more appropriate?

It is helpful here to look at the concept of deep and surface learning. The individual version of this concept has been expounded by Gibbs (1992) in his studies of undergraduate teaching and learning. In surface learning the focus is on the acquisition of facts, skills and concepts, memorising these and reproducing them to demand in examinations or demonstrations. By contrast, deep learning consists of looking for patterns, relating knowledge, skills and concepts to specific contexts, and seeking to understand and apply rather than merely recall or demonstrate.

In studies of school management, Miles (1987) identifies a similar notion as a major distinguishing feature of transformational leadership – transformational leaders possess a 'deep coping' ability. Surface coping consists of rapid, intuitive, reactionary responses to changes in the environment; deep coping, however, requires a rational review of the significance of the environmental change as against the general strategic intent of the organisation and thence a proactive response. Deep coping means being 'in tune' with the tide of history and the evolving life cycle of the organisation.

Obviously, surface and deep coping are not merely alternative ways of conceptualising the task of leading and managing organisations and although transformational leaders need to have a capacity for deep coping, all leaders need to be able to surface cope. The trick is knowing which to use and when and this requires an understanding of change which embraces evolutionary (incremental/life-cycle) as well as revolutionary (chaos/conflict/complexity) approaches. Lepani's (1994) work on the long waves of history and the new learning society is a masterly exposition of such thinking.

Swieringa and Wierdsma (1992) build on Argyris and Schön's (1974) similar notions of single and double loop learning (single loop learning can be equated to organisational surface coping and double or triple loop learning to organisational deep learning) to identify four types of learning organisations:

- **Prescriptive organisations** change slowly through the application of tried and tested rules and bureaucratic procedures. Thinking and learning goes on away from the process of production or service by 'staff' departments such as personnel, finance and research and development (see Figure 2.4).

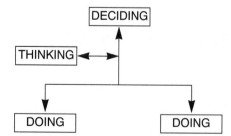

Figure 2.4: Thinking and learning in prescriptive organisations
Source: Swieringa and Wierdsma, 1992. Reprinted by permission of Addison Wesley Longman Ltd.

- **Entrepreneurial organisations** cope with rapidly changing environments by rapid intuitive reaction – they don't really have time to think, individually or organisationally! (see Figure 2.5.)

Figure 2.5: Thinking and learning in entrepreneurial organisations
Source: Swieringa and Wierdsma, 1992. Reprinted by permission of Addison Wesley Longman Ltd.

- **Unlearning organisations** are aware that a surface approach through minor adjustments is unlikely to satisfy future contexts and therefore they engage in whole-organisation reviews and audits to prepare themselves for a paradigm shift (see Figure 2.6).

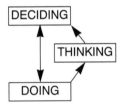

Figure 2.6: Thinking and learning in unlearning organisations
Source: Swieringa and Wierdsma, 1992. Reprinted by permission of Addison Wesley Longman Ltd.

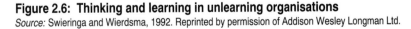

- Finally, **learning organisations** accomplish the paradigm shift but they also acquire the capacity for going through the whole process again, setting up long-range environmental scanning facilities to monitor when a future 'cusp point' might be approaching requiring further reengineering (see Figure 2.7).

Much of the literature on reengineering assumes all organisations are at the 'sigmoid curve' transition point and therefore a fundamental rethink is required to avoid stagnation and decline in order to realign the business process to better satisfy the needs of the customer. If this is, indeed, the case then a full reengineering job probably is necessary. Megatrend analysis, millennium fever and the collapse of the Eastern bloc would indicate we may well be at such a 'cusp' point in Western economies, hence therefore the appropriateness of the reengineering approach. However, the 'white heat' of

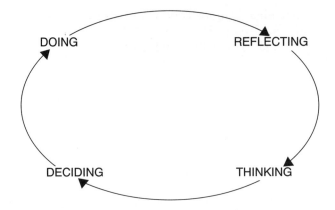

Figure 2.7: Thinking and learning in learning organisations
Source: Swieringa and Wierdsma, 1992. Reprinted by permission of Addison Wesley Longman Ltd.

contemporary technological and politico-economic change may well blind us such that we are unable to perceive the subtleties of evolutionary change and thus the need for surface learning, consolidation and regrouping.

Implications for schools

As we approach the tenth anniversary of the publication of the National Curriculum consultation document, it seems an apposite time to look back, with the benefits of hindsight, and begin to apply some of these techniques.

Interestingly, there is a time lag between teachers' awareness of the position on the life cycle and the actual position – for example, it took some time for schools to begin to see all the initiatives in the Education Reform Act 1988 as a single package of related issues and thus realise the need for fundamental reengineering. Paradoxically, many schools are just now regrouping for major change when, it could be argued, we are in a period of incremental development in the Dearing five-year moratorium period.

On the other hand, experience suggests that, in order to achieve the review of the National Curriculum due by the turn of the century, we ought to be starting now so that we hit the transition point on the sigmoid curve and through reengineering the curriculum prepare more appropriately for the challenges and opportunities of the next millennium.

In contrast, the Teacher Training Agency's proposals for an integrated and coherent set of National Standards for key points in the teacher's career (TTA, 1996), can be seen as a framework describing what is already good practice in a large number of schools and LEAs. However, the legal and financial arrangements for creating both a national framework and an open market for professional development is very much seen as a fundamental change for the providers of INSET and staff development, so what is incrementally developmental for schools (at this stage) may well be a reengineering issue for higher education.

This dilemma illustrates the complexity of applying life-cycle analyses in the real world of the school, let alone determining the appropriate learning style. In practice, each aspect of the school (subject areas, pastoral groupings, development plan initiatives, local and national priorities) will be at a different point on the life cycle and the teachers will be operating in different learning modes (individually and as a group). However, this is not so very different from the product provision analysis which commercial organisations would carry out. Each product (or service) would be analysed according to a range of indicators and its position on the life cycle determined to ensure an overall balance of products at different life-cycle stages and thus make sure that the company's products (or services) weren't all, for example, at the initial stages of development or reaching old age at once. Of course, there would also be a whole organisation summary which would be a gestalt of the individual product/service position.

In summary, in order to begin to take a learning organisation approach to improvement, the school would need to use the wide range of information available about courses, sections, initiatives, individuals and teams to determine the life-cycle stage and therefore appropriate learning style for participants. In one sense this is parallel to using a variety of teaching and learning strategies with pupils from a knowledge of their skills, abilities and past results. Certainly, a school which was a mature learning organisation would have satisfied the key conditions outlined by Garratt (1990, pp. 78–9) as well as working in the ways identified by Holly (1994, pp. 132–6) but other schools will be working towards this position and thus may be using other strategies for organisational learning which are more appropriate for their stage of development.

Conclusion

The key to becoming any type of learning organisation, therefore, is for its leaders to be aware of the stage of development of the various sections and programmes and thus what the school's overall position is in the life cycle. There are a large number of indicators which can be used to determine this but it is the action taken as a result of this analysis which distinguishes whether the school has the capacity to become a mature learning organisation. This entails a focus on learning at all levels and an appropriate balance between surface (or single loop) learning and deep (or double/triple loop) learning.

Using Swieringa and Wierdsma's (1992) types of learning organisations we might postulate the following as a rule of thumb for relating organisational learning to environmental change:

Contexts when **surface** or incremental learning might be best:

Organisational type	**Environment of change**
• entrepreneurial	rapid, non-paradigmatic change
• prescriptive	slow predictable change

Contexts when **deep** learning or a reengineering approach might be best:

Organisational type	**Environment of change**
• unlearning	sigmoid curve, pre-paradigmatic
• learning	new mind-set, post-chaotic cusp

Given the increasing focus on leadership development and management learning in the business and public sector, surely now is the time for school leaders to recapture their position for leading learning, not only for their own staff and schools, but also in partnership with their peers in the community? We may then stand some chance of bringing about the lifelong learning goal of learning individuals in learning organisations for a learning society.

Having examined the organisational aspects of learning, the next chapter will look at professional learning from the perspective of the individual. Part II will then use these conceptual tools to develop a range of practical techniques and approaches to individual and organisational learning and, through the examination of a number of case studies in good practice, identify how a sample of schools, LEAs and nations are approaching the task of continuing professional development for lifelong learning.

3
∎ ∎ ∎

Professional Learning

It is, perhaps, one of the ultimate ironies of the professional development of teachers that it should take up so much time, cost so much and yet be of uncertain efficacy. A clue as to why development is so uncertain when it comes to demonstrable outcomes is the confusion and ambiguity which surrounds the epistemological status of training and development. The two concepts ebb and flow in usage and seem entirely interchangeable. It is possible to detect in usage an implicit hierarchy of significance in which 'training' is related to specific skills, 'development' to a broader, less tangible process and 'education' (in a professional context) to a longer-term heuristic process.

Very rarely are these various terms subsumed under a comprehensive definition of how professionals actually learn. This is entirely understandable as many schools have only a limited perception of how their pupils learn. The historic, and continuing, emphasis has been upon the teaching process with a naïve faith that there is a necessary and contingent relationship between teaching, the learning of the individual and her or his capacity to act and apply that learning.

This chapter explores the focus that might be significant in formulating a model of professional development that is posited on learning. The chapter examines three main areas:

- the context of professional learning;
- the components of professional learning;
- developing a model of professional learning.

The context of professional learning

This section sets professional learning in context by demonstrating its relationship to the various components of organisational development and improvement and illustrating that fundamental improvement in schools is the result of individual learning.

The issue is best demonstrated by Fullan (1993):

> *Teachers (and all of us) should think of change and innovation as they would about their own lives. Life (and change) is not always moving forward, bad things happen beyond our control, fortune shines on us unexpectedly etc. etc. That is life. But, and this is the key, some people cope better, and even thrive, while others fall apart. The very first place to begin the change process is within ourselves . . . Therefore, teachers should look for their first lessons from individuals who do a better job of learning even under adverse circumstances. (p. 138)*

The important point here is that individual learning, and so understanding and the capacity to act, is the essential prerequisite to any attempt at organisational development and improvement. Unless reform is rooted in individual learning then it can only ever be superficial, fragile and transient. How many innovations have appeared to be initially successful in terms of changes in behaviour only to founder and wither because they had not become systemic? There is substantial evidence to indicate a high correlation between profound professional learning and successful improvement, change, the creation of a learning organisation and the evolution of a model of consistent practice across the whole school.

Professional learning and school improvement

In their 11-part typology of the characteristics of effective schools Sammons *et al.* (1995) identified the notion of the learning organisation, i.e. school-focused staff development, as a fundamental characteristic. In their analysis of the factors influencing school improvement Stoll and Fink (1996) argue:

> *Staff development can be misapplied, however, unless it is understood in relation to the meaning of change and the change process. 'One-shot' strategies are of little assistance. Staff development strategies within the school . . . have all been found to aid classroom and school improvement. (p. 58)*

The 'meaning of change' and the 'change process' are directly related to personal understanding, individual perception and the capacity to change behaviour rooted in a fundamental shift in a person's conceptual map. This latter point is powerfully reinforced by the National Commission for Education (1996). In their report on schools succeeding against the odds they note:

> *Most of the accounts suggest that it is not essential to have new staff to create a new ethos in the staff room, and vigorous staff development had been used in preference to the replacement of teachers. Successful approaches involved knowing how to develop or 'grow' staff capabilities, and acknowledging, in effective operational terms, the importance of non-hierarchical team work . . . (p. 343)*

It seem axiomatic to argue that the achievement of school effectiveness, improvement or success is directly correlated to staff development. What is important is that the relationship is seen to exist and relates to individual change more than to generic training.

Managing change

Change is fundamentally and profoundly about learning – the two are linked in a way that makes them symbiotic. Personal change, for example in a new relationship, is a function of learning to respond appropriately and effectively to one's partner. Organisational change is about developing the generic capability to work in a new context and so in new ways. Personal and organisational change is very much about shifting cultural norms and expectations.

Culture is the most elusive and intangible of concepts and yet it is fundamental to organisational development and improvement. As Rosenholtz (1991) found in her research:

> When teachers conversed in either moderate or low consensus schools, they stressed students' failings instead of their triumphs perhaps to avenge themselves of the day-long strain imposed on them. In high consensus schools, by contrast, shared goals, beliefs, and values led teachers through their talk to a more ennobling vision that placed teaching interests in the forefront, and that bound them, including newcomers, to pursue that same vision. (p. 39)

In other words a common, shared culture was found to be an essential pre-requisite to the creation of a learning environment focused on pupil success. This view is reinforced by Rosenholtz's findings about teacher learning:

> In learning-enriched schools, teachers tended to hold a sustained view of their learning ... When we asked teachers to identify sources of their professional renewal, those in learning enriched settings primarily cited colleagues in conjunction with their own problem-solving and creative capacities ... (ibid., p. 103)

Pupil success would appear to be, at least partially, the results of a success-focused culture and that culture is, *inter alia*, the result of a perception by teachers of themselves as learners:

> The extent of teachers' learning opportunities increased the performance gains of one cohort of youngsters in both reading and maths over a two-year period, regardless of pupil–teacher ratio or the extent of teachers' professional training. (ibid., p. 103)

The creation of an appropriate and valid culture in a school is the result of the interaction of a wide range of variables of which one of the most significant is the extent to which teachers are learning. Teacher learning has the effect of helping to create such a culture and is a crucial and significant manifestation of that culture. However, Fullan and Hargreaves (1992) offer a cautionary note:

Understand the school and its culture before changing it! *Put priority on meaning before management. (p. 113)*

Meaning is the way in which culture is exemplified. The implementation of change is fundamentally about the realignment of meaning and this in turn occurs through learning.

The learning organisation

This topic has been discussed at length in Chapter 2. At this stage it is simply necessary to restate the importance of the relationship between organisational learning and individual learning. The essential characteristics of the school as a learning organisation may be summarised as:

- a public commitment to the learning of every individual;
- creating a learning partnership with all stakeholders;
- centring all management processes on the enhancement of human potential;
- operating in a culture of continuous improvement, development and growth.

Fundamental to these four points is a recognition that the learning organisation is made up of learning individuals. Organisations of themselves do not learn; it is the willingness and capacity of the individuals that are the members of the teams that make up the organisation that create the potential to improve through learning.

Schools that are learning organisations are characterised by:

- an explicit requirement for all members of the community to be engaged in learning;
- as much confidence about learning as there is about teaching;
- systematic review and reflection as essential constituents of every process;
- high significance attached to learning, recognised through systematic praise and reinforcement.

Consistent practice

An issue which is difficult to prove empirically but has significant weight anecdotally is the extent to which the way in which teachers are led and managed is a model for the relationship between teachers and pupils. Much of what emerges from our understanding of the nature of the learning organisation points to the need for symmetry in all aspects of organisational life. Fundamental to the core purpose of the school, students' learning, is the notion that those who are responsible for student learning should also be learners themselves – not just subject experts but people who make mistakes, are anxious, fail, are exhilarated by understanding and filled with awe when something new is discovered.

It is difficult to conceive of true learning taking place unless everyone involved experiences what it is to learn. The issue for professional learning is therefore far more than providing functional knowledge and skills – it is to model and exemplify and so reinforce a culture of learning. It is worth speculating on the extent to which adult learning in schools is subject to the same levels of failure as student learning. What is being argued for here is for harmony and integrity. A useful concept in this context is that of 'self-similarity'. Derived from complexity theory it helps us to understand fractal relationships – that no matter what the scale patterns and relationships remain the same. There needs to be self-similarity in learning – the learning of every individual in a microcosm of the whole and there is a clear and discernible pattern emerging when all experiences are aggregated.

The purpose of this first section has been to contextualise the issue of professional learning – to argue that its significance is much more than instrumental, rather it has to be understood as a fundamental component of every aspect of the way in which a school is managed. Just as it is argued that there is no situation in which a pupil will not be learning (even if that learning is essentially negative) so there can be no situation in which the adults in a school cannot be learning. It is difficult to conceptualise of any aspect of school life which is not entirely and fundamentally dependent on learning. However, given the elusive status of the concept it is necessary to explore it in greater depth.

The components of professional learning

The first need in this section is to reflect on the use of the term professional learning. The use of 'professional' in this context is problematic. Although widely used by teachers as both a description and an aspiration in strict sociological terms, the teaching force probably does not meet all the criteria for professional status. Bottery's (1994) analysis of the characteristics of professionals produces the following criteria (based on pp. 116–17):

1 The existence of a body of unique and systematic knowledge.
2 The requirement for considerable technical skill.
3 A lengthy period of training.
4 The need to reflect on and improve practice.
5 The ability to respond to complex situations.

6 The existence of a high degree of personal autonomy.

7 Selection, training and qualification is controlled by the profession.

8 There is one authoritative professional body.

9 There is a monopoly of provision by this body.

10 Discipline is exercised by the profession.

11 A crucial social service is provided.

12 The occupation enjoys high social prestige.

13 There is a high level of remuneration.

14 The profession is highly involved in policy making.

15 There is an ethic of service.

16 There is a code of ethics.

17 Training involves socialisation into the ethics.

Clearly many of these criteria are problematic if applied to teachers. Some (1, 2, 3, 4, 5, 6, 11 and 15) are clearly applicable, others are less so and some are not relevant. It is perhaps significant that the first category is directly relevant to this book. Numbers 15, 16 and 17 are also relevant in this context, although more often implicit and contentious. It is not intended in this context to enter the debate about graduations of professional status (semi-, para-, etc.) but rather to argue that the appellation professional is useful in the context of professionalism. A professional is someone who seeks to apply the principles of professionalism to the way they work. In this usage professionalism is not concerned with social status, governance or remuneration but rather with the morality which determines how the work is done, i.e. intention and delivery are subject to higher-order significance.

Just what this signifies in education remains contentious and subject to a wide range of claims. For most teachers the principles are probably broadly encapsulated in their school's aims or mission statement. Although these range from pious banality to outrageous assertion there is a consensus about the overarching purposes of education:

- the maximisation of potential;
- the enabling of learning;
- the creation of a safe environment;
- the provision of an appropriate curriculum;
- responsiveness to stakeholders;
- personal and social development.

The permutations of this list are endless but they do represent a purpose. Working in a morally consistent way towards that purpose might be described as professionalism – those who do so might be described as professionals. It is with this understanding that this discussion continues.

If the notion of professional is complex then that of learning is even more so. A great deal of the writing about the nature and purpose of education operates in a deficit mode when it comes to learning. This is particularly true when it comes to the learning of pupils (see Bowring-Carr and West-Burnham, 1997); few schools have an explicit, shared definition of learning let alone a learning policy. Discourse is in terms of teaching and the curriculum rather than the learning process. The ambiguity about pupil's learning is reflected, and may be symptomatic of, equal ambiguity in terms of professional learning. If schools are to move towards being learning organisations in which everybody is viewed as a learner then the artificial dichotomy between teacher and taught has to go. As Darling-Hammond (1997) points out:

> *Teachers learn just as their students do: by studying, doing and reflecting; by collaborating with other teachers; by looking closely at students and their work; and by sharing what they see. This kind of learning cannot occur solely in college classrooms divorced from engagement in practice or solely in school classrooms divorced from knowledge about how to interpret practice. (p. 319)*

Although what follows will tend to refer to teachers it should be read as applying to the full staff of the school and many of the principles are also transferable to student learning.

Andragogy

Andragogy is the theory of learning as applied to adults – it stands in contra-distinction to pedagogy, theories of teaching applied to children. The validity of this distinction is highly contentious and in the context of schools may actually be counter-productive. The creation of a hierarchy of meaning with regard to learning has significant dangers as it can only serve to reinforce the notion of children being dependent learners and thereby diminish their potential for achievement. At the most basic level it is worth questioning at what stage in a person's development do they cease to be a 'child' learner and become an 'adult' learner. The answer is, of course, that it varies with the individual. It will also vary with the knowledge or skill to be learnt.

It may well be that the andragogic model is the most appropriate for any learner. What is needed in schools is a holistic and integrated approach to learning which recognises and respects the individual and demonstrates consistency in relating learning strategy to individual need, irrespective of age.

In his careful and comprehensive review of the psychological factors influencing adult learning Tennant (1997) provides an eclectic model which reconciles the key strands of psychological analysis. In what he calls a 'reconstructed charter for andragogy' he identifies eight characteristics (pp. 140–1):

- valuing the experience of learners;
- engaging in reflection on experiences;
- establishing collaborative learning relationships;
- addressing issues of identity and the power relationship between teachers and learners;
- promoting judgements about learning which are developmental and which allow scope for success for all learners;
- negotiating conflicts over claims to knowledge and pedagogical processes;
- identifying the historical and cultural locatedness of experiences;
- transforming actions and practices.

Set in the context of professional learning in schools these characteristics allow a number of principles to be derived. First, there has to be a profound respect for, and tangible recognition of, the integrity of the experience of the individual. All too often developmental activities are offered out of context – assuming a homogeneity on the part of those to be developed and thereby diminishing their own histories. This recognition has to be coupled with enhancing the status of prior experience by encouraging reflection on it so as to clarify and confirm its status and to identify an appropriate starting point for development.

Second, there has to be an understanding of the nature of the relationship between teacher and learner. The semantics of this relationship are complex as it is almost impossible to use language that does not imply some kind of power relationship, the perpetuation of a dependency culture and the control of access to knowledge and skills. Hierarchical relationships are endemic to education, and status and perceived significance are often the key determinants of the design and delivery of professional development programmes. The delivery of expert knowledge in an authoritative manner may be interesting and enjoyable (especially for the presenter) but it is doubtful if it bears any real relationship to learning.

Third is the issue of the status of knowledge. One of the major problems with the improvement of educational practice in Britain is that it is so tightly specified and defined by statute. An Act of Parliament does not facilitate the creation of a professional interpretative community nor the development of a postmodern critique of policy. This inevitably has the effect of compromising any debate about the epistemological status of policies relating to classroom practice or school management. And yet, as in any arena of human activity, multiple interpretations are possible and, given the significance of education, desirable. This is not to argue for total relativism but rather to argue that the learning process requires the possibility of varying perspectives and that these should be reconciled through intellectual rather than authoritarian processes.

Finally, adult learning has to facilitate success expressed through action. This is not to diminish the importance of challenge, nor to deny the possibility of failure, but rather to stress that the design of any learning programme should have as a fundamental axiom the enhancement of the individual's capacity to change her or his behaviour if that is the appropriate outcome. How many middle management and deputy heads' courses have been compromised by the observation 'This is great, but I wish my head was here to hear this'? Professional learning has to be designed around implementation as well as knowledge and skills.

It is worth reiterating that nothing that has been postulated in this section is not equally applicable to the design of learning experiences of young people.

Converting learning into practice

One of the key issues to emerge from the previous section is the importance of the relationship between the choice of developmental activities and the desired outcome. One of the most important pieces of research carried out in this area is that of Joyce and Showers (1988). The focus of their research was the relationship between the various components of training and the impact on job performance. The central issue was the efficacy of transfer between training and changes in outcome. The outcomes of their research are shown in Figure 3.1 in the very useful typology developed by Wallace (1996).

What is dramatically clear from Wallace's presentation of the results is that high impact and high transfer only occur when the full range of training components are deployed. The crucial element is that high transfer of training

Training components and combinations	Impact on job performance		
	Knowledge	Skill	Transfer
Theory	Low	Low	Nil
Theory and demonstration	Medium	Medium	Nil
Theory, demonstration and practice	High	Medium	Nil
Theory, demonstration, practice and feedback	High	Medium	Low
Theory, demonstration, practice, feedback and coaching	High	High	High

Figure 3.1: Training components, their combinations and impact on job performance
(Based on Joyce and Showers, 1988; Wallace, 1996, p. 24)

only takes place when coaching is added to the equation. Knowledge and skills can both be adequately provided for using the first four components but it is only when theory, demonstration, practice and feedback are actually located in the job itself and coaching is available that the purpose of training is actually realised. The full implications of this model are described by Wallace:

> *Presentation of theory and demonstration of good teaching according to this rationale give a basis for initial conceptualising and observation while practice, feedback and coaching provide opportunities for experimentation, concrete experience and reflective observation using the concepts of the theory. (p. 24)*

This analysis can be seen as a profound critique of much of the provision for professional learning. Many courses offer high quality provision of the first two elements, a number make the second two components available but very few programmes are able to provide all five components in a coherent, systematic and sustained manner. The practical implications of these findings will be considered in Chapter 6. Here the next important concept to clarify is that of coaching.

Coaching and reflection

Coaching and reflection are combined in this section because of their pivotal status in translating training into learning and so into improved practice. It is possible to argue that without coaching and reflection learning cannot in fact take place – there is simply a superficial response in which knowledge and skills might be displayed but there is no profound understanding and so no fundamental, and lasting, change in behaviour.

Coaching can probably be best described as a 'helping relationship'. Analogies with sports training are, for once, helpful and appropriate. The sports coach helps the athlete by

- observing performance;
- analysing that performance;
- measuring performance against standards;
- identifying remedial and/or reinforcing strategies;
- evaluating those strategies against changes in performance;
- consolidating improvements.

In the same way the professional coach works with the teacher, manager or student to facilitate progression. Central to the coaching relationship is the high quality of personal and inter-personal skills and the development of mutual trust, confidence and respect. The essentially hierarchical nature of schools has tended to equate coaching with a line-management function, and this could prove to be highly inappropriate if not actually dysfunctional. Although there is a very high probability that seniority and experience will have developed the necessary skills and qualities it doesn't automatically follow. The sensitivity of the coaching relationship is fundamental to the success of any learning outcome. According to Argyris and Schön (1974):

> As individuals come to feel more psychological success and more likelihood of mutual confirmation or disconfirmation, they are likely to manifest higher self-awareness and acceptance, which leads to offering valid information, which again leads to feelings of psychological success ... As individuals feel higher degrees of freedom of choice, trust and authenticity, they are more likely to test their assumptions publicly, which is, in turn, likely to enable others to feel higher degrees of freedom of choice ... (pp. 91–2)

However powerful and effective the learning relationship is, it is unlikely to have a profound impact if it is not rooted in personal reflection, which Knowles (1993) defines as:

> ... an intra-personal process through which personal and professional knowing can occur. Reflection is seen as a process and method of informing practice with reason. Reflection is not seen as static; implicit in its meaning is action. It is seen as a vehicle for promoting changed behaviours and practices, and as a means of improving foresight, lessening the chances of taking inappropriate lines of action. (p. 83)

The exhortations to reflect are very strong – the practice is much more complex. Chapter 5 will examine the components of reflection as part of professional learning in practical terms. At this stage it is worth highlighting the following issues:

1   Reflection has to become implicit to professional practice, it has to be seen as a constituent of every process.
2   Reflection has to be modelled in whole-school procedures and processes – monitoring, review and evaluation are the organisational equivalent of personal reflection.
3   Equally, reflection has to be a component of student learning and there has to be a shared expectation that the outcomes of reflection will be seen as significant and acted on.
4   Reflection requires support in terms of materials and strategies to aid the process and a coach to support and facilitate the process.
5   Time for reflection is obviously crucial but this does not necessarily mean the timetabling of 'Reflection Time'; rather it should be made intrinsic to every process, e.g. lesson planning and review, the professional development review process, target setting, etc.

A powerful conceptual model that gives a theoretical underpinning to the notion of a learning relationship is Vygotsky's (1962) view of cognitive development. An individual's cognitive growth is a function of their *appropriating* (or taking up) and *internalising* the culture in which they exist.

Development can only take place through the mediational sign system, the most significant aspect of which is speech. Cognitive development takes place through discourse between the learner and the helper. As Vygotsky believed that development is culturally rather than biologically determined it is the actual relationship that serves as the catalyst for growth. In discussing the capacity for growth Vygotsky introduces the concept of the *zone of proximal development*. He defines this:

> ... as the difference between a child's actual development level as determined by independent problem solving and the higher level of potential development as determined through problem solving under adult guidance or in collaboration with more capable peers. (1978, p. 86)

Although he was writing about children the concept of the zone of proximal development has significant implications for the sequence of learning. Three stages are discernible:

1 The learner's problem-solving activities are regulated by the 'other'.
2 The learner assumes responsibility for the problem-solving process by actively redefining the problem.
3 The problem-solving activity becomes self-regulated.

This sequence is a perfect conceptual model of the relationship between coach and client, rooted as it is in a developmental progression towards internalisation and so understanding and thus autonomy. The zone of proximal development also raises the important issue of knowing where the client is and then adopting a systematic strategy to realise the maximum potential in any given area of skill or knowledge. What is also important is that the process of mediation is appropriate to the individuals involved and the task undertaken.

Coaching and reflection are inextricably linked – the purpose of both is to facilitate the process of internalisation and so develop understanding and thereby the capacity to act autonomously. Awareness of the *nature* of the coaching relationship, the means of *communication* that it employs and the *stages* through which it develops are essential components of its success. The use of coaching in professional learning will also serve as a powerful model for student learning; as Darling-Hammond (1997) argues:

> When faced with learning demands that stretch them to the edge of their developing capacities, students must also have access to substantial coaching to support their progress and to ensure they will be motivated to succeed rather than intimidated into failure. Clear standards must be coupled with sustained supports. Teachers must work in settings structured to enable close, continual relationships. Personalisation is not just 'nice' for students; it is essential for serious teaching and learning. (pp. 106–7)

For 'student' substitute teacher and for 'teacher' substitute leader.

Praxis

Central to any discussion of professional learning has to be a recognition of the importance of the evidence of appropriate praxis. The purpose of professional learning is to enhance practice which is evidenced by the learning of students. The discussion in this section so far (i.e. coaching, reflection, the research of Joyce and Showers) has had at its heart professional activity. Professional learning only has meaning to the extent to which the practice of the art or skill of teaching is extended.

However directly or indirectly, professional learning has to be related to the actual tasks, jobs, etc. that have to be done. The most appropriate model of this relationship is based on Kolb's (1984) learning cycle (see Figure 3.2).

The starting point is 'concrete experience' – actually doing the job, practising the skills, displaying the artistry. This is followed by the process of understanding and reflection which in turn facilitates the formulation of abstract conclusions which are then tested and may be incorporated into future practice. The process is dynamic and iterative.

If professional learning is to improve practice then it has to be designed in such a way as to facilitate each stage of the Kolb learning cycle but has to be firmly grounded in actual, real tasks. This has resulted in what is usually understood as action learning. McGill and Beaty (1995) define action learning as follows:

> *Action learning is clearly not about gaining bits and pieces of knowledge nor about memorising – it involves the person as a complex whole acting in the world. Action learning therefore supports the view of learning that is about development and understanding in relation to the world rather than separate from it. Thus learning in action is holistic and developmental. It integrates learning from experience with learning with ideas through the process of reflection. (p. 175)*

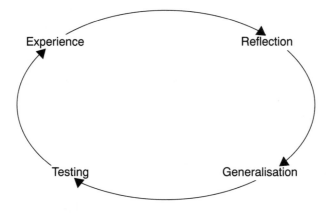

Figure 3.2: The learning cycle
(After Kolb, 1984)

The best known manifestation of this approach in schools is action research which has a distinguished, if somewhat limited, pedigree. The holistic purposes of action research are captured by Hargreaves (1995) when he argues that there is a need to create a:

> collective professional confidence that can help teachers resist the tendency to become dependent on false scientific certainties ... by replacing them ... with the situated certainties of collective professional wisdom among particular communities of teachers. (p. 153)

Pollard and Tann (1993, p. 9) argue that a research-based approach in teaching has the following characteristics:

1 It is concerned with aims and consequences as well as means and technical efficiency.

2 It is applied in a cyclical or spiralling process in which practice is subject to continuous review and revision.

3 Skills in the review and research process are seen as integral to any model of teacher competence.

4 The personal qualities of open-mindedness, responsibility and whole-heartedness are fundamental to the process.

5 Judgements about professional activity are derived from self-reflection *and* insights from theoretical disciplines.

6 The process of action-based learning is enhanced through social interaction and dialogue.

Dewey (1929) (quoted in Skilbeck, 1970) captures the essence of professional praxis:

> The practitioner who knows the system and its laws is evidently in possession of a powerful instrument for observing and interpreting what goes on before him [sic]. This intellectual root affects his attitudes and modes of response in what he does. Because the range of understanding is deepened and widened he can take into account consequences which were originally hidden from view and hence ignored in his actions. Greater continuity is introduced ... his practical dealings become more flexible ... He is emancipated from the need of following tradition ... he has a wider range of alternatives to select from in dealing with individual situations. (p. 160)

In the final analysis, as Dewey states, 'Education is a mode of life, of action' (p. 163). If professional learning is not rooted in action then a valid and appropriate praxis will not emerge.

Learning styles

All learning is essentially individual, subjective and idiosyncratic. This part of the discussion of professional learning focuses on two aspects of the individualisation of learning. Although there may be instances where a generic approach is appropriate (e.g. in the conveying of information), by definition it is unlikely any learning will actually take place – awareness might be raised in some instances. In order to increase confidence that professional learning is actually taking place a range of variables have to be taken into account of which two of the most significant are learning styles (after Kolb, 1984) and multiple intelligences (Gardner, 1984).

Honey and Mumford (1986) have shown how each stage of the learning cycle can be related to a preferred mode of learning. They have identified four distinct learning styles – activist, reflector, theorist and pragmatist – and their work with the diagnostic tool they developed, the Learning Styles Inventory, indicates that individuals may have one dominant learning style. The significance of this becomes clear when the attributes of each type of learner are defined:

- **Activist:** focuses on the task itself, seeks to avoid the other elements, gives highest significance to the job.
- **Reflector:** naturally disposed to review and analyse but may have difficulty translating the outcomes of reflection into plans.
- **Theorist:** most comfortable working with the abstract, good at establishing cause and effect but relatively poor at deploying understanding.
- **Pragmatist:** quick to plan and to 'get on' with things.

No person has one of these characteristics to the exclusion of others. However, there may well be a preponderant characteristic which will have a significant impact on the relative capacity to learn in different circumstances. There are four significant implications of the learning styles approach for professional learning:

1 The design of professional development activities has to take into account the varied learning styles of participants.
2 Individuals need to be aware of their own learning style in order to manage their own development programme.
3 The learning cycle and the learning styles associated with it need to inform routine processes in schools, e.g. the planning and delivery of lessons, the management of teams, meetings and projects.
4 Individuals need to understand their own learning styles profile in order to enhance their capacity in those areas where they are relatively 'weak'.

Learning styles are not a panacea but they do provide an opportunity for the individual to take greater responsibility for their own learning.

A very different approach to understanding an individual's preferred mode of learning and their capacity to learn is provided by Gardner (1984). His work on multiple intelligences is proving to be one of the most significant insights into the management of learning to have emerged in recent years. To date there has been no substantial attempt to relate the concept of multiple intelligences to professional learning – what follows is tentative. If Gardner's proposition 'that there is persuasive evidence for the existence of several *relatively autonomous* human intellectual competencies' (p. 8) is accepted and the notion that professional learning should model student learning is also accepted then a number of implications follow.

First, there is a need to relate the multiple intelligences to the various domains of professional activity. In *Frames of Mind* Gardner identifies the following intelligences:

- linguistic
- musical
- logical – mathematical
- spatial
- bodily – kinematic
- inter-personal
- intra-personal.

To this list Gardner has recently proposed the addition of naturalistic intelligence (awareness of the natural world) and existential intelligence (personal understanding of the spiritual or transcendental). Although the relative significance of each intelligence will vary according to context and role, there can be no denying the relevance of the various intelligences to professional activity. What Gardner (1993) sees as the purpose of school could also be the purpose of professional learning:

> ... *to develop intelligences and to help people reach vocational and avocational goals that are appropriate to their particular spectrum of intelligences. People who are helped to do so, I believe, feel more engaged and competent ... (p. 9)*

Second, Gardner's (1993) view of the implications of multiple intelligences for the work of educators has interesting implications for the management of professional learning. He argues for:

1 assessment specialists to diagnose 'abilities and interests';
2 student–curriculum brokers '... to help match students' profiles, goals and interests to particular curricula and to particular styles of learning' (p. 10);
3 school–community brokers to 'match students to learning opportunities in the wider community' (p. 11).

Gardner also sees a role for a 'master teacher' whose job would:

> ... *involve, first of all, supervising the novice teachers and guiding them; but the master teacher would also seek to ensure that the complex student–assessment–curriculum–community equation is balanced appropriately. (p. 11)*

There is nothing in this model that is alien to the notion of professional learning. In fact the principle of 'balancing the equation' is at the heart of all learning and could be seen as *the* management and leadership issue for schools. Gardner goes on to provide a specific example of the application of multiple intelligences to the learning of students which again has resonances for professional learning:

> ... *most productive human work takes place when individuals are engaged in meaningful and relatively complex projects, which take place over time, are engaging and motivational, and lead to the development of understanding and skill. (p. 224)*

In considering the implications of multiple intelligences for schools Gardner (1993) 'insists' on four elements (p. 207):

1 The goal of an education that is geared to understanding.
2 A stress on the cultivation of performances of understanding, which can be assessed primarily in context.
3 A recognition of the existence of different individual strengths.
4 A commitment to mobilise these productively in the education of each child.

Multiple intelligences is still a long way from acceptance as an alternative view of intelligence in the organisation of pupils' learning, and therefore even further from integration into models of INSET and professional development. However, it does offer significant insights into the formulation of a model for professional development.

Teachers as intellectuals

Giroux (1988) raises a central issue in any definition of professional learning – what is the purpose of such learning and how should this inform its nature? Chapter 1 has already referred to the trend towards the reduction of the role of teachers, managers and leaders to an instrumentalist view where it can be delivered in terms of competencies. Giroux's concern is that this process results in teachers becoming:

> ... *the object of educational reforms that reduce them to the status of high-level technicians carrying out dictates and objectives decided by experts far removed from the everyday realities of classroom life. The message appears to be that teachers do not count when it comes to critically examining the nature and process of educational reform. (p. 121)*

Giroux identifies a number of specific trends centred on 'bureaucratisation', the development of 'instrumental ideologies', the 'standardisation of school knowledge' and the 'devaluation of critical, intellectual work on the part of teachers and students' (pp. 122–3). His rejoinder to these trends is to argue for teachers as 'transformative intellectuals'. Central to his argument is that by:

> *viewing teachers as intellectuals, we can illuminate the important idea that all human activity involves some form of thinking ... by arguing that the use of the*

mind is a general part of all human activity we dignify the human capacity for integrating theory and practice, and in doing so highlight the core of what it means to view teachers as reflective practitioners. (p. 125)

The creation of such a perspective challenges the functional approach to pedagogy and also raises the issue that educational choices, whether national policy or classroom based, do not permit simple rationalistic decisions. All educational activities are matters of value that require active participation in order to enhance the quality of decision making and obtain commitment and involvement. It is not possible to argue that the purpose of schools is to create autonomous, critical thinkers if teachers are not included in the proposition.

The conditions that are appropriate for teachers to function as intellectuals are very similar to those of any group of learners. In essence they can be reduced to the following:

- open access to information and knowledge;
- recognition that information and knowledge are the products of cultural norms;
- a culture of analysis and critical thinking;
- acceptance of alternative modes of functioning;
- respect for the integrity of individual perspectives.

Most of these factors can be created through the management of professional learning. Two issues predominate. First is the extent to which professional learning is presented in an authoritarian manner, seeking to prescribe 'right answers' or is offered in a cautious, tentative way. Second is the availability of higher-order cognitive techniques focusing on critical analysis and the development of judgements.

The latter point raises the issue of cognitive skills. The contribution of cognitive skills enhancement to pupil performance is increasingly understood. Its role in professional learning is less clear. The deployment of cognitive skills in the classroom is probably a direct correlation of the extent to which teachers experience their use in their own learning and development.

A cognitive curriculum, for both teachers and students, might include the following topics (Perkins, 1992, pp. 103–4):

- Levels of understanding ... kinds of knowledge 'above' the level of content knowledge in their abstraction, generality and leverage (e.g. problem-solving strategies).
- Languages of thinking ... verbal, written and graphic languages that assist thinking in and across subject matters.
- Intellectual passions ... feelings and motives that mobilise the mind towards good thinking and learning.

- Integrative mental images ... that tie a subject matter or large parts of it together into a more coherent and meaningful whole.
- Learning to learn ... building students' ideas about how to conduct themselves most effectively as learners.
- Teaching for transfer ... so that students use in other subject matters and outside of school what they learn in a particular subject matter.

Perkins argues that these elements combine to form a meta-curriculum. Such a meta-curriculum for professional learning might include the following specific topics:

- inductive and deductive logic
- critical thinking
- creative thinking
- comparative analysis
- problem solving
- contextualization
- generalization.

If these specific intellectual skills are combined with what Said (1994) describes as the true function of the intellectual then the role of the teacher is powerfully enhanced:

> The intellectual today ought to be an amateur, someone who considers that to be a thinking and concerned member of a society one is entitled to raise moral issues at the heart of even the most technical and professionalized activity as it involves one's country, its power, its mode of interactivity with its citizens as well as with other societies. In addition the intellectual's spirit as an amateur can enter and transform the merely professional routine most of us go through into something much more lively and radical; instead of doing what one is supposed to do one can ask why one does it, who benefits from it, how it can reconnect with a personal project and original thoughts. (p. 83)

Professional learning has to be about much more than increasing technical efficiency – its primary purpose is the creation of understanding of the moral, social and cultural context in which learning takes place. This is not to deny the relevance of very specific and practical skills and competencies but rather to argue that they have to be contextualised.

Conclusion: developing a model of professional learning

On the basis of this first part of the book it is possible to identify a number of criteria to inform the subsequent discussion of the specific components of professional learning. Although each criterion has significance in its own right we would argue for the cumulative impact. It is recognised that the movement away from staff development, training days and INSET is a slow one, and that many schools are already implementing a professional learning approach – the issue is the creation of a holistic and systematic view which permeates every aspect of work in the school and is not another thing to be managed by somebody with an additional role.

Any systematic approach to professional learning should take the following elements into account:

1 There has to be a clear and explicit link with a school improvement strategy and integration with relevant management processes, i.e. strategic and development planning, target setting, etc.

2 Professional learning has to be expressed through a learning policy which embraces all members of the school community.

3 Individual and organisational needs have to be reconciled recognising the equal integrity and validity of both.

4 Individual learning programmes have to be designed on the basis of negotiated diagnosis.

5 Professional learning has to be focused on the actual work of the individual and on their capacity to grow and develop.

6 Any external provision should be planned so as to reinforce and integrate with internal provision.

7 All professional learning should serve as a model, an exemplification of best practice for the learning of students.

8 Professional learning needs to be focused on research-based, problem-solving critical and analytical studies.

9 Wherever possible professional learning should be team based and team processes should be designed to facilitate learning.

10 Coaching has to become the most significant working relationship in the school.

11 Individual learning styles and intelligences should be diagnosed, understood and respected.

12 Professional learning has to focus on an intellectual appreciation of what it means to be an educationalist as well as instrument training.

13 The management of professional learning itself should be the subject of reflection, review and evaluation.

14 Professional learning has to be as concerned with the whole person (social, emotional and physiological) as well as with the employee.

PART TWO

■ ■ ■

Approaches to
Professional Learning

4
■ ■ ■

Techniques for Effective Professional Learning

One of the most important aspects of managing professional learning is the choice of appropriate techniques to facilitate and support learning. Unless there is a high correlation between a number of variables the possibility of learning taking place is significantly diminished. This chapter explores the nature of those variables and then describes a range of techniques, activities and strategies which are appropriate to the model of professional learning outlined in Chapter 3.

The relevant variables and the relationship between them are shown in Figure 4.1.

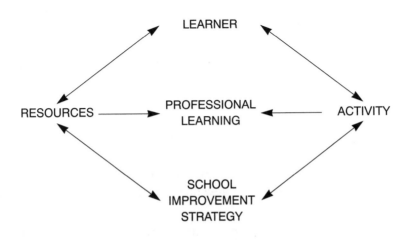

Figure 4.1: The variables influencing professional learning

Each variable in the diagram can be elucidated thus:

- **Learner:** the individual in terms of her or his:
  - experience
  - motivation
  - learning style
  - perceived needs
  - role
  - development strategy.
- **Activity:** the type of professional learning technique that is available and appropriate.
- **Resources:** using the term in its broadest sense, i.e.
  - time
  - colleagues
  - expertise
  - finance.
- **School improvement strategy:** individual development programmes will only be organisationally meaningful if they are produced in the context of an explicit, known, shared, understood and accepted whole-school strategy.

Managing the process of choosing the right activity is a complex one and is highly significant in that the chances of optimising professional learning are a direct correlation of the extent to which the activity is valid and appropriate. Central to the review of techniques that follows is the Joyce and Showers (1988) model discussed in Chapter 3 (see p. 51) and their notion of the probability of *transfer* taking place, i.e. that the activity actually impacts on practice. Traditional professional development activities can have a wide range of outcomes of which learning to create understanding to improve practice is often the most elusive. It is perhaps significant that it is very difficult to find research documentation that demonstrates the extent to which developmental activities actually work. There are abundant reports of levels of satisfaction with training events themselves but confident assertions about transfer and changes to practice are more elusive.

The strategies described in this chapter are designed to increase confidence that intention is translated into action.

Action research

Action research has the potential to combine many of the features outlined in Chapter 3 as the prerequisites of professional learning. Hitchcock and Hughes (1995) define action research thus:

> *The principal features of an action research approach are* change *(action) or collaboration between researchers and researched. Action researchers are concerned*

to improve a situation through active intervention and in collaboration with the parties involved ... the end of such research is not simply the contribution to knowledge, but practitioner-relevant information. (p. 27)

In terms of practice the salient features of action research are:

1 Focus on a specific issue or situation.
2 Practitioner driven and managed.
3 Improvement as the outcome
4 Democratic or collaborative processes
5 Eclectic and functional use of research methodologies.
6 Functioning through reflection-in-action.
7 Pragmatic use of theoretical perspectives.
8 Contextually specific conclusions.
9 Integration of values and practice.
10 Corroboration and validation by peers.

Because the research is 'owned' by the practitioner(s) it is not subject to the same constraints as a more formal research activity. At the same time it has to meet a range of criteria which are common to those in 'public' research. The issue of research ethics remains the same as does the relationship between the generation of data and the drawing of inferences. Validation is significant as, although the research is specific and local, it can represent a significant contribution to professional understanding and so should be shared. Lomax (1994) identifies the dangers in action research as:

where issues are not sharply delineated; where the focus is one-sided and oversubjective; where the researcher is unaware of projection; and where there is insufficient outsider involvement to compensate for possible insider collusion, that is, where practitioners have a vested interest in getting a specific outcome. (p. 166)

Cohen and Manion (1980) identify eight stages in action research to increase confidence in its validity:

1   The identification and formulation of the problem, project, issue or topic to be researched.
2   Identifying and negotiating with the possible participants and stakeholders and the possible formulation of a contract.
3   Investigation of comparable studies in the literature.
4   Modification or realignment of the focus of the research.
5   Choice of research methods and agreement of roles.
6   Identification and implementation of appropriate review, monitoring and evaluation procedures.
7   Implementation of the project:
    −   collection of data

- monitoring and review
- classification and analysis of data.

8 Collation and interpretation of data – development of conclusions, implementation of any changes, evaluation of the project.

To Cohen and Manion's list a ninth category has to be added:

9 Identification of the next topic for improvement.

If action research is not a continuous process then there is a danger of it becoming an 'academic exercise' in the worst sense. The loss of formal rigour in terms of research is compensated for if there is evidence (a) of real improvement through change which is dealing with the real issues and (b) evidence of teachers becoming more reflective, developing a portfolio of skills and accepting personal responsibility for improving learning processes in their classrooms.

Examples of the sorts of topics that are appropriate to an action research approach might include:

- investigation into the effectiveness of different approaches to the teaching of reading;
- analysing the impact of different assessment strategies on pupils of differing ability levels;
- evaluating a new strategy, e.g. coaching and its impact on examination performance;
- monitoring the effectiveness of the implementation of a strategy derived from outside the school, e.g. reading recovery or assertive discipline;
- investigating gender differences in the usage of information technology;
- reviewing the impact of a health education programme on drug abuse;
- monitoring parents' perceptions of changes in reporting and consultation procedures;
- evaluating different approaches to managing team processes.

What action research offers is a professionally valid technique which enhances teacher efficacy in the actual process of work and therefore does not diminish, or detract from, the core purpose. In this sense it is highly cost-effective and congruent with the notion of teacher as learner accepting personal responsibility for improvement. A further significant benefit is the potential to improve social relationships and enhance professional co-operation.

Autobiography

Autobiography has the potential to be a powerful source of reflection, a way of clarifying meaning and, perhaps most importantly, a means of affirming the significance of an individual's experience. In the context of professional learning autobiography is perhaps too generic a term. What is intended is a piece of highly personal reflective writing which focuses upon a specific aspect of an individual's working life. Thus there might be a number of autobiographies, each relevant to a particular theme, e.g.

- career evolution and planning;
- personal educational values and goals;
- the evolution of teaching and learning strategies;
- attitudes towards special educational needs.

Of course autobiographical writing can be much more general and be almost exclusively concerned with recording personal feelings and emotions about the full gamut of an individual's life. It might take the form of an intellectual history, a personal journey towards professional understanding, etc.

Clearly such writing is highly personal and might be considered too sensitive to be of value for professional learning. However, under the writer's control reflective writing can be used with a coach or mentor as well as help the individual to clarify and order experience and perceptions. This process is one of 'social constructivism' which Claxton (1996) argues is:

> ... the sense that people make of their experience is a function of the knowledge, beliefs, schemes and attitudes, derived from previous, culturally situated experiences, that they bring with them to the new event. Those knowledge structures which are brought to bear are the source of the personal meaning that that experience has. Meaning is constructed by the person and attributed to experience ... (p. 10)

Autobiographical writing in the context of professional learning can help the learner:

- prepare for a needs analysis review;
- respond as an equal partner in a coaching/mentoring situation;
- contextualise courses and programmes;
- make sense of most professional learning techniques.

Most importantly perhaps it is a crucial component of any reflective activity, notably the journal. It can also serve as a useful model for developing similar strategies with pupils as an aid to their becoming more reflective learners. Self-knowledge is an essential attribute of the effective learner. As Covey (1989) expresses it:

> Because I am self-aware, because I have imagination and conscience, I can examine my deepest values. I can realise that the script I'm living is not in harmony with those values, that my life is not the product of my own proactive design, but the result of the first creation I have deferred to circumstances and other people. And I can change. I can live out of my imagination instead of my memory. (p. 105)

Award-bearing programmes

The place of award-bearing programmes in professional learning is complex. They represent one of the most substantial areas of activity in terms of time, cost and energy. Yet their relationship to school improvement, classroom effectiveness and personal development remains problematic. This is largely explained by the fact that many programmes have to respond to a range of criteria that are determined by imperatives other than those of school improvement, e.g.

- the need to cover the academic courses in terms of content;
- the demand to be comparable with similar academic programmes;
- concern about academic standards, particularly through modes of assessment;
- the need to market programmes in terms of their generic appeal and the related issue of cohort viability.

These factors explain some of the concerns about higher education programmes discovered by Glover and Law (1996, p. 70). They found the perceived disadvantages of HE provision (in descending order of significance) to be: travel time and time lost, costs, university staff being 'out of touch' and remote from reality, 'off-the-shelf' programmes and variable quality.

The central issue is one of remoteness – in terms of geography, relevance and awareness. There is also the problem of the perceived relationship between theory, research and practice. Almost by definition professional practitioners attribute high significance to their own practice and that of colleagues whom they trust and respect. Often this practice will assume a superordinate status when compared with, or challenged by, other practice as represented by research findings. Equally with theory there is often a high degree of caution about its relevance and significance – especially when it is expressed at a high level of cognitive abstraction. This is probably a valid and understandable response.

If these concerns are placed in the broader context of the motivation of teachers in following an award-bearing programme, which may often be primarily in terms of personal career development, then the potential for professional learning is inhibited. In reviewing the advantages of higher education provision Glover and Law (1996) found the following number of mentions for each category:

Research base	5
Staff expertise	4
Staff/ideas up to date	3
A different viewpoint	7
Good quality overall	7
Negotiated content	3

Accreditation	6
School improvement focus	2
Total mentions	37

The relative weightings for accreditation and school improvement may be significant in understanding some of the issues incorporating higher education provision into a model of professional learning which is focused on school improvement. Recent years have seen substantial changes in the design and delivery of award-bearing programmes. The characteristics of 'leading-edge' provision include:

1 The recruitment of a homogeneous cohort in terms of professional experience and developmental needs.

2 The identification of individual learning strategies, the negotiation of learning contracts and the use of diagnostic review to design a programme of study.

3 Negotiation of content, especially the recognition and respect of participants' prior learning and experience.

4 Sessions that focus on challenge, critical thinking and problem solving rather than information transfer.

5 Opportunities for systematic and continuous reflection.

6 Assessed outcomes that are work focused and negotiated in terms of content and presentation.

7 The use of the cohort as a formal and informal resource – especially for networking.

8 The use of a wide range of resources for learning.

Many programmes of study meet these criteria although the relationship between the acquisition of a diploma, masters degree or doctorate and enhanced classroom or school performance remains problematic. Of course there is a case for advanced study which focuses on pure as opposed to applied knowledge, and of course individuals have the right to obtain personal, career-enhancing recognition for their learning. This is especially true when people are having to pay for their own courses of study. However, in terms of effectiveness, it does seem that the pursuit of an academic award can be a lost opportunity for both the individual and the school.

If a higher degree programme is to enhance an individual personally and professionally then a number of personal characteristics are important. In her discussions of EdD (Doctor of Education) Student and Staff experiences Hall (1996, p. 182) identifies a range of 'learning repertoires':

- making their own decisions;
- choosing to do what they want rather than should;
- loving knowledge for its own sake;

- preferring collaboration to competition;
- being ambitious intellectually rather than vocationally;
- reflecting on their own learning and teaching;
- respecting and wanting others' expertise;
- relating knowledge to practice;
- being determined not to fail.

These characteristics have strong echoes of the criteria for professional learning identified at the end of Chapter 3. They can also be applied, without any modification, to any learning situation that goes on in a school.

Award-bearing programmes can help to provide insights, foster under-standing, translate knowledge into practice and support the creation of a critically inquiring professional community. They can also support the notion of the teacher-as-intellectual, not because of the 'level' of the work being done but because of the higher-order thinking that is encouraged and the broader vision that hopefully emerges.

Coaching

The term coaching is deliberately chosen and has to be seen in contradistinction to mentoring. Mentoring may be seen as being primarily concerned with listening, understanding and aiding reflection. Coaching, by contrast, is much more concerned with practice and implies active intervention. As was argued in Chapter 3 professional learning is fundamentally about enhancing the capacity of the individual to do her or his job. Joyce and Showers (1988) have demonstrated that coaching is the crucial determinant of improvement in performance. It therefore follows that for most developmental activities coaching has to be a fundamental component of the overall design.

In the context of this discussion coaching can be said to have the following characteristics. It is:

- focused on improving job performance;
- based on diagnosis, analysis and reflection;
- centred on high-quality interpersonal relations;
- concerned with target setting;
- about recognition, reinforcement and praise.

Coaching is a helping process designed to translate understanding into actual practice. It is very much about perceptions, negotiating, understanding and then identifying strategies, implementing them and reviewing change. The analogy of sports coaching is appropriate and helpful here. The improvement of any skill or technique follows a simple process:

- What can I do now?
- What do I want to be able to do?
- What actions do I need to take?
- Have the actions worked?

The role of the coach is to ask the questions, help to set the targets, advise on the actions, help to review progress and, perhaps most importantly, to consolidate success. Sporting analogies are always dangerous but a significant feature of most sports coaches is that they are not actually better performers than those they are coaching – often quite the reverse. The authority of the coach is not derived from experience *per se* but rather from skills and qualities to help another understand their experiences. These skills and qualities may be identified as:

- active listening to ensure genuine understanding
- empathising and showing genuineness
- providing accurate feedback
- confronting negativity
- analysing performance
- acting as a source of information
- offering encouragement and support
- creating opportunities
- critically reviewing options
- helping to create a picture of ideal performance.

This list might appear to be a counsel of perfection – there simply cannot be enough people with these skills and qualities available in any school. However, learning to become an effective coach is a professional learning activity like any other – best done through school practice. The coaching relationship is an interactive one. It grows and matures through sophisticated interaction and review – how the relationship develops is as important as what it is trying to achieve. Coaching involves a very high degree of reciprocity with the coach learning as much as the client. This obviously argues against a formal, hierarchical relationship. Although many coaching relationships are based on the coach having 'superior' status in terms of experience or authority (and can work very well), in a learning environment it is inappropriate to see this as the most significant criterion for matching coach and client. Experience and authority are no guarantees of skills and qualities. In many circumstances it may well be that peer (or near-peer) coaching is the most effective model.

The capacity to 'help' in the context of clear criteria for performance is perhaps the most significant component of coaching. It may well be that in many cases self-selecting pairings are going to be the most effective. For example, a newly qualified teacher may well be best helped by someone who has recently gone through the same experience – similarly for a newly appointed head of department, deputy or headteacher.

Finally it is important to raise the issue of the interaction between adult and pupil learning in the school. It has already been argued that how adults learn is a powerful model for how they work with young people. There is significant evidence that coaching is a powerful factor in raising pupil achievement:

> *Most reading schemes based on an interventionist approach require one-to-one relationships. The most successful work with children with emotional or behavioural difficulties is on an individual basis. Many schools have found that coaching is the most powerful way to improve performance in public examinations ... (Bowring-Carr and West-Burnham, 1997, p. 98)*

Coaching of pupils is likely to be most effective when it is carried out in a school that has a culture of coaching. Teachers obviously need to coach young people but pupils are often expert when coaching other pupils. Coaching therefore becomes implicit in every working relationship – everyone is coached and everyone coaches. In particular, anyone who has a leadership function has coaching as a primary function in their job description or equivalent. This is not an additional task but rather a better way of managing the essential purpose of teaching and managing – enhancing performance. The permutations of the coaching relationship are almost endless – the following examples provide some indication of the possibilities:

- a newly qualified teacher in the first year of teaching;
- a deputy head preparing for a headship interview;
- a maths teacher preparing to introduce a new maths scheme;
- a science teacher being helped with strategies to support literacy;
- an 'apprentice' timetabler;
- a teacher studying for a Diploma in Special Educational Needs;
- a newly appointed lunchtime supervisor;
- a head of department studying for a Masters degree by distance learning;
- a sixth-former who will be coaching Year 7 pupils in reading.

Coaching has often been seen as alien to a professionally staffed organisation – it can be perceived as impinging on professional autonomy because of its interventionist nature. However, it will only work if it is based on reflection, which is highly personal, and is carried out with appropriate respect and based on trust – these are highly professional characteristics.

Courses and conferences

It is interesting to speculate just how much time, energy and money has been invested in teachers attending courses and conferences and how much impact they have had on classroom practice and leadership and management effectiveness. Two problems emerge directly from this. First, we just do not know – there is a lack of real data. Second, there would appear to be enormous inconsistency in the relevance and applicability of courses and conferences. Reference has already been made to the model developed by Joyce and Showers (1988); their analysis of the components of training and their relative effectiveness would seem to indicate that by definition most courses and conferences can only make a limited contribution to professional learning.

The problem of transfer is exemplified in the evaluation sheets that are used in many courses – they are issued and completed at the end of the event, and tend to focus on the suitability of the venue, domestic arrangements and levels of satisfaction with the day itself. Rarely do they feature issues of transfer and implementation. Courses which are external to the school (school-focused training days are discussed below) can be likened to orbiting the earth in a Space Shuttle. The prevailing sensations are a detachment from reality, distance lending enchantment to the view, and a sense of being cocooned. When the time comes to return to earth the angle of re-entry has to be exactly right otherwise the vehicle is either burnt up in a hostile atmosphere or skids off into outer space doomed to emit increasingly incoherent messages. A safe landing depends on a sophisticated supportive infrastructure.

Courses and conferences may well serve valid and useful purposes in raising awareness, stimulating interest and motivating. If this is the stated intention then they are valid in their own terms. But given the anxieties about shortage of resources and the potentially disruptive impact on pupils' learning then the validity and integrity of such experiences has to be questioned. There is a complex equation which has to be reconciled in order to justify attendance at any externally provided course or conference. The following checklist can be applied when reviewing the appropriateness of attending an externally provided course:

1 How far does the course coincide with the needs analysis of the person attending?

2 How consistent are the course outcomes with the School Development Plan and targets for improvement?

3 Are the course aims and objectives expressed as learning outcomes?

4 What strategies does the course offer for support and implementation?

5 Is the course the optimum means of obtaining the knowledge, skills, etc.? (Is there nobody in the school with the knowledge and skills?)

6 Are the course organisers and presenters the best and most appropriate people?

7 What learning strategies will be used on the course?

8 What will be the costs in terms of fees, travel, supply, etc.? Is there a more cost-effective alternative?

9 How will the outcomes of the course be disseminated in the school?

10 Who is the most appropriate person in the school to provide coaching and support?

Not all the issues raised by these questions are applicable to all courses and conferences but in the final analysis the question has to be: is your journey really necessary?

Distance learning

Distance learning, largely through the Open University, has been a significant factor in the professional development of teachers for nearly 30 years. The model that has emerged – high-quality learning resources, tutorial support and assessment focused on the individual's work needs – has helped to set standards in terms of quality provision. The advantages of using distance learning approaches are well understood:

- flexibility in studying
- minimum disruption to work
- access to state-of-the-art resources
- cost-effectiveness
- accreditation.

Schools have used distance learning packages to provide the resources for in-house training and development programmes. Well designed resources and materials can be employed to support a bespoke programme. Significantly a number of schools have found distance learning programmes to be of value in providing or augmenting A level provision. It may well be that as costs continue to rise distance learning will become increasingly cost-effective and part of the provision of learning materials in most schools. The continuing impact of information technology makes it probable that the quality and provision of materials will continue to rise. The emphasis that the Teacher Training Agency is placing on multimedia presentations of its programmes represents a substantial shift in this direction.

The constraints on any distance learning programme which includes accreditation are the same as those for any award-bearing course – the issues of relevance and transfer. However, in this context it may well be that the 'medium is the message' – the process of using IT and other multimedia approaches can help to prepare teachers to work in a different way to facilitate pupil learning.

In order to meet the criteria for effective learning distance learning programmes need to be:

1 incorporated into school development strategies;

2 'customised' into the specific context;

3 supported by coaching and an action learning set;

4 capable of practical implementation.

Distance learning programmes that have up-to-date course materials, activities and exercises that are more than comprehension checks and provide opportunities for collaborative problem solving offer some of the most significant opportunities for enhancing professional learning.

Experiential learning

One of the biggest problems in any formally designed learning activity is what Hall (1996) refers to as readiness and willingness – you can send a teacher to a course but you can't make them learn. The learning potential of any programme will always be a function of motivation which will in turn determine the impact on the individual and so transfer to their work.

Experiential learning has long been seen as a strategy for managing the problem of impact. Wallace (1996) defines experiential learning as learning where:

> The emphasis is on active engagement of learners, the primacy of their learning experience, facilitation (as opposed to transmitting knowledge), and making sense of experience through reflective dialogue between facilitator and learner. However, no distinction is made between different kinds of experience and the degree to which they relate to the context in which the learning is designed to be used. (p. 19)

It is the important insight of this last sentence that raises the central issue with experiential learning, the extent to which the learning is applicable. One of the problems with experiential learning is that it is often perceived to involve bizarre activities involving the great outdoors, usually in January and almost certainly including getting wet – great fun perhaps but not always related to actual work and often undertaken in the absence of key colleagues who have not shared the experience, the language and so do not necessarily subscribe to the learning outcomes.

Wallace goes on to discuss Schön's (1987) view of the 'practicum' which Schon defines as:

> a setting designed for the task of learning in practice ... The practicum is a virtual world, relatively free of the pressures, distractions and risks of the real one to which, nevertheless, it refers. (p. 37)

The virtual world of the 'practicum' is exemplified most graphically in the flight simulator – the situations are real enough to induce physiological changes but there is never any risk. In terms of professional learning most educators will have encountered some form of simulation – from the banality of the 'in-tray' exercise to the potential power of the micro-teaching situation. Wallace argues (p. 23) that the essential issue is one of transfer, and that this is an issue of learning design – as per the Joyce and Showers model. Coaching appears to be the only vehicle to facilitate the switch from the 'virtual' to the 'real' world.

The ever-increasing sophistication of IT and multimedia approaches means that it is becoming much easier to create valid and significant simulations that learners will recognise and accept the validity of. One of the most important opportunities offered by a practicum is the chance to explore the implications of a decision in depth, through to its logical conclusion. Much military training is now in terms of computer simulated scenarios which allow options to be explored and then reviewed and analysed in detail. It is doubtful whether training in education will ever receive the financial resources of the military or civil aviation but the models are available.

At one level role-play can be seen as a form of practicum but it is usually difficult to create situations where participants invest the activity with sufficient significance to make it a valid learning experience. What is clear is that experiential learning through a practicum meets many of Kolb's criteria for learning and has reflection and coaching at its heart. The biggest constraint on this approach is that the organisation to which the learner returns may not be managed to sustain and apply the learning that has taken place. Experiential learning depends, more than most strategies, on the existence of a learning organisation.

Job enrichment

To offer an overworked and under-rewarded teacher the opportunity for job enrichment might appear to be adding insult to injury. However, in the context of professional learning and personal career development there are few more fertile areas to encourage growth. In essence job enrichment in the redesigning of a job to increase the opportunities for developing new skills and knowledge. The job has to be redesigned so that the new tasks provide opportunities for growth, challenge, recognition, a sense of achievement and, most importantly, a feeling that valid learning is taking place. A fundamental prerequisite of job enrichment is the identification of a coach who has a primary duty to ensure that learning is taking place and that the expansion of the job is not another example of 'delegation by dumping'.

Job enrichment can take two broad forms, horizontal and vertical. In horizontal enrichment a greater number of tasks at the same level of responsibility and authority are taken on. Vertical enrichment involves the taking on of greater responsibility and authority. Of course it is possible to combine the both. Over the past few years most teachers have seen an increase in their responsibilities (if not their authority) because of the demands of the National Curriculum. In order to avoid a sense of imposition or overburdening the following stages need to be followed in setting up a job enrichment programme:

1   There has to be a developmental motivation that is not expedient or resource driven.
2   A coach must be identified at the outset.
3   A learning contract must be drawn up based on analysis of the existing job, specifying the additional levels of responsibility and authority and identifying the developmental support required.
4   Links with any externally provided training need to be established.
5   Timescales need to be agreed together with appropriate outcomes in terms of learning, career development and, if appropriate, salary.

Job enrichment is a good example of an opportunity to begin to move the culture of a school away from delegation and empowerment to providing real opportunities for autonomous leadership. The crucial issue is the amount of authority that is made available – leadership implies the capacity to act and genuine development can only take place where the potential to learn exceeds the inhibitions of bureaucratic accountability.

Examples of job enrichment in practice could include:

- a young teacher leading a project team on the development of a learning policy for the school;
- the science co-ordinator assumes responsibility for a whole-school IT strategy;
- a deputy represents the school on an LEA working party;
- form tutors are given the authority to make direct contract with parents on matters of academic progress and discipline;
- a head and her or his deputies rotate responsibilities *and* authority to act.

Whatever type of enrichment activity is identified it is vital that it is a 'real' job and that the experience gained is built on, developed and incorporated into a personal strategy for professional learning in the context of school improvement.

Professional clinical review

Clinical review is a technique found in hospitals and research communities where an individual explains the circumstances surrounding a particular incident or event and is then questioned by others to clarify the circumstances. This approach might be used following an unexpected death, the failure of a proven technique, the success of a new approach. The purpose is to increase and share understanding.

In a hospital setting a clinical review might involve the protagonist(s) – medical staff, nurses, technicians, administrators, etc. – in fact anyone who was involved or had an interest in the topic. A presentation is followed by questioning, clarification, proposal of explanations, drawing of conclusions and agreement of future practice. It is described here as a professional clinical review in order to stress:

- the focus on practice, not the person;
- a collaborative, non-confrontational approach;
- the pooling of collective wisdom;
- the identification of best practice;
- the emphasis on future practice.

At its best this technique has the potential to encourage reflection, foster collaboration and consolidate experience. The process is one of analysis, no blame and respect for all perspectives. Although potentially intimidating for the individual(s) this technique offers a highly sophisticated model to support learning and school improvement. Its application in schools might include:

- review of a department's success in public examinations;
- disseminating the outcomes of an action research project on the use of IT for assessment;
- analysing the strategies employed with a group of pupils with learning and behavioural difficulties;
- sharing the results of a programme using accelerated learning techniques;
- evaluating parental dissatisfaction with a consultation evening.

The clinical review can be a powerful stimulus to learning, enhance professional relationships and integrate reflection, theory and practice. It is also intellectually and personally challenging, requiring rigour and high-order cognitive skills.

Reflective practice

It is central to this book that reflection and coaching are the keys to effective professional learning. They are also fundamental to the development of leadership qualities and potential. However, reflection remains elusive as a concept and difficult to describe in terms of actual practice.

Reflection is the process of giving meaning to, and so understanding, experience. The means by which understanding is achieved will include analysing, categorising, prioritising, contextualising and, crucially, interpreting. Huczynski (1983) quotes Dewey (1909) who defined reflective thought as the:

> ... *active, persistent and careful consideration of any belief or supplied form of knowledge in the light of the grounds that support it and the further conclusions to which it leads. (p. 209)*

Gardner (1984) approaches this issue from the context of multiple intelligences where he discusses the notion of a 'sense of self' which is:

> ... *an emergent capacity. It is a capacity that grows initially out of the intrapersonal* and *the interpersonal intelligences ... [which leads to] the devising of a* special kind of explanatory model *encompassing everything that the individual is and everything that the individual does.*

> ... *human beings ... are able to take the inchoate understanding that lies at the core of intrapersonal intelligence and make it public and accessible to themselves ... (pp. 296–7)*

It is the development of the 'explanatory model' that is crucial to the understanding of self and so to the ability to communicate that understanding and then act on it. However, it is difficult to conceptualise what people actually do when they reflect – it has to be more than 'thinking about' which could be cursory, dismissive or uncritical. Reflection implies an image being returned and that holds the clue to the process. Although reflection is a personal and subjective process, to work it needs objectification. The process of reflection requires a stimulus in the form of a consolidated and internalised experience, an appropriate questioning process and a means of comparing that experience against other sources.

Any experience has validity in the context of reflection, the issue is the selection of specific experiences to provide a focus for learning. The development of a focus through the process of needs analysis is dealt with in Chapter 5.

The ability to ask the right question is a key skill in reflection. In many situations it will be the coach who has the responsibility for generating valid and appropriate questions. Notwithstanding this responsibility, the person reflecting needs a personal inventory of diagnostic questions, e.g.

- What were the circumstances that led to _____?
- What was my contribution to _____?
- What did other people contribute?
- Why did _____ develop in the way it did?
- How does _____ relate to my previous experience?
- How did my skills and knowledge contribute to _____?
- How did I respond intellectually/emotionally?
- Why did I respond in that way?

- How does this experience compare with _____?
- What have I learnt about _____?
- What have I learnt about myself?
- What do I need to do to _____?
- Who do I need to talk to about _____?
- What can I offer others?
- How do I consolidate this experience?
- What additional skills and knowledge do I need?
- What have I learnt about my own learning?
- How do I improve?

The efficacy of these questions will be significantly enhanced if they are asked in the context of alternative sources and interpretations. A number of strategies are available of which the three most apposite in an educational setting are keeping a journal, reading and observation.

Journal

The keeping of a reflective diary or journal is a well established strategy. The term 'journal' is used to emphasise the reflective nature of the writing rather than a simple chronological narrative. Keeping a reflective journal is very much a matter of personal style but certain guidelines may be helpful:

- journal entries should be made on a regular basis;
- a range of styles can be used for entries: critical incidents, a thematic narrative, responses to reading, dialogues with a coach, etc.;
- entries could be structured in terms of:
  - a narrative describing a situation
  - analysis and reflection
  - planning and target setting;
- there should be a summative review at regular intervals to consolidate learning and provide a framework for the next stage of development.

The journal must obviously be confidential. Many who have kept such a journal have found that it also develops a therapeutic value, a way of coming to terms with a complex and demanding job.

The journal can be used in conjunction with a reading strategy, with significant extracts from books, the educational press, etc. being copied into the journal and used as the basis for reflective writing. Some of the best reflective writing starts with a brief factual account which is followed by a relevant piece of published writing which inspires a stream of consciousness narrative exploring issues, options, feelings and responses. This is then followed by more systematic analysis and, if appropriate, target setting. There is a danger that keeping a journal can create a dependency culture – it becomes addictive. However, the notion of any practitioner spending 30 minutes a week reflecting is hardly indulgent – it may be essential to personal survival and professional growth.

Observation

Reflection and coaching both require data and evidence to provide the impetus for review, to answer the question 'where am I now?' and to ensure a realistic and valid appreciation of actual practice. Unfortunately for many teachers observation has negative connotations – as an assessed component of teaching practice, as part of an imposed appraisal scheme with elements of accountability, as an element of OFSTED inspections and as part of capability procedures. Although individual experiences will obviously vary the professional provenance of appraisal is not good.

A further issue concerns the status of the data collected through observation of teaching or management tasks. In essence there will always be an element of artificiality, of contrivance, if nothing else because of the presence of a non-participant observer. Just as the presence of a research anthropologist will disrupt the rituals of the society being studied so the observer will inevitably distort what is being observed. A fundamental proposition of the uncertainty principle is that 'you cannot measure without changing'. The evidence from observation has to be treated with great caution if for no other reason than the observer is in a superordinate position to the observer. Issues of hierarchy may well be the dominant factor, power and control being the most significant determinants of the outcome.

To support reflection, to facilitate the work of a coach and to be consistent with the principles of professional learning any data-gathering process has to be:

- based on negotiated perspectives;
- part of a continuous process, not an arbitrary 'one-off';
- cognisant of the contingent nature of any conclusions drawn;
- derived from multiple perspectives – not just the observer and the observed but also the participants.

Reading

Reading is often regarded as an essentially solitary and passive activity. An often heard comment by teachers on award-bearing programmes is that 'It has forced me to read again.' Professional reading is often one of the first casualties of teachers who have too much to do, are tired and need to devote what limited spare time there is to personal refreshment – not books like this one. The place of reading in learning is captured by Manguel (1997):

> In every literate society, learning to read is something of an initiation, a ritualised passage out of a state of dependency and rudimentary communication. The child learning to read is admitted into the communal memory by way of books ... (p. 71)

Reading gives the reader access to autonomous understanding and enhances their capacity to communicate. Reading as part of a structured programme has the potential to support the growth of individual understanding, to enrich the world-view, to create a more sophisticated mental map and to deepen the process of reflection. Significantly a number of reading schemes for children require that the teacher also reads, a further example of pupil learning and teacher learning being harmonised.

Every professional teacher needs a reading strategy (possibly managed through the journal) to aid personal reflection, to be a stimulus to dialogue with their coach and possibly to support shared discussion with team members. What follows is a biased, subjective and opinionated list of some of the titles that someone aspiring to a leadership role might consider as parts of their reading strategy:

Bowring-Carr C, and West-Burnham, J. (1997) *Effective Learning in Schools*, Pitman.

Davies, B. and Ellison, L. (1996) *School Leadership for the 21st Century*, Routledge.

Drucker, P. (1993) *Post-Capitalist Society*, Harper.

Gardner, H. (1995) *Leading Minds*, Basic Books.

Mulgan, G. (ed.) (1997) *Life After Politics*, Demos.

Nair, K. (1994) *A Higher Standard of Leadership*, Berrett-Koehler.

National Commission for Education (1996) *Success Against the Odds*, Routledge.

Senge, P. (1990) *The Fifth Discipline*, Doubleday.

Sergiovanni, T. (1996) *Leadership for the Schoolhouse*, Jossey-Bass.

Sun Tzu (1988) *The Art of War*, Shambala.

Wheatley, M. (1992) *Leadership and the New Science*, Berrett-Koehler.

Zeldin, T. (1994) *An Intimate History of Humanity*, HarperCollins.

This list obviously represents a particular perspective on leadership – it might be argued that it does not matter what is read as long as reading is taking place and is responded to. Reading is an essential characteristic of the teacher and leader as intellectual. There is nothing more ennobling and empowering than literacy, there is nothing more developmental than the use of literacy to enhance understanding.

Reflection requires a mirror. Understanding comes from the clarity of the image – not 'through a glass darkly' but through as rich a picture as it is possible to create.

Shadowing

Shadowing is a developmental activity where one colleague follows or tracks another in the course of their normal working day. At its most minimal it is a means of obtaining information about the content of the shadowed person's work. Thus it can help to clarify the nature of the job, identify the skills and knowledge required to do it and possibly help the person doing the shadowing if that type of work is for them.

A variant of this model is the shadowing of someone outside the organisation – industrial placements are an obvious example. In this case the learning is likely to be through comparison and contrast, e.g. comparing the work of the head of department in a secondary school with that of a section leader in a large retail store. Shadowing can be a one-way process – the shadower simply watches and forms a view of the job being observed. However, if the process becomes reciprocal then it begins to develop more of the characteristics of coaching. In these circumstances shadowing needs to meet the following criteria:

- It is an active rather than a passive project.
- There are clear learning outcomes established.
- While retaining the 'ordinariness' of the job being observed the observer is able to experience the distinctive features of the role.
- There are opportunities for analysis and reflection.
- The experience is supported by coaching and leads, if appropriate, to changes in the observer's job.

In the context of school improvement a more significant use of shadowing is perhaps the shadowing of pupils. Although this has the same potential for artificiality as any form of observation, this is overcome by the enhanced possibilities of what it actually means to be taught and to learn and to be a member of the school community. The insights into the realities of pupils' experiences may provide the most salutary feedback as to the extent to which the school's intentions and values are actually translated into everyday experiences.

There is always the danger of shadowing being, at worst, voyeuristic and at best 'interesting'. If it is seen as a technique for increasing understanding through reflection supported by coaching then it can generate powerful learning.

Teaching as learning

It is often argued that the best way to learn and understand a topic is to teach it. A major barrier to this stratagem in the context of professional learning and development might be described as 'fear of failure'. Credibility and authority are so often seen as being equated with success that it requires significant confidence to engage in a topic where one is primarily a learner rather than having the reassurance of the subject authority of the teacher. The success of learning through teaching will obviously be a significant function of the culture of the school, and in particular of the quality of personal relationships.

A common use of teaching as learning which combines effective learning and development for the individual with a cost-effective use of resources for the school is the teaching of the content of a course that the individual has attended. This strategy, when it works, combines enhancing the understanding of the presenter with dissemination and so can enhance the status of both the individual and the topic.

A variant on this theme is the notion of the 'teaching partnership'. Two teachers form a partnership which might be expressed through reciprocal coaching, a joint research project or mutual observation on an agreed topic. In this instance teaching becomes learning through a critical friendship focused on classroom practice or management behaviour. Wallace (1991, pp. 49–50) identifies the following advantages of this approach:

- providing confidential mutual support;
- providing informal support;
- encouraging reflection and providing emotional support.

There seems little doubt that one of the most powerful ways to help teachers enhance their performance is to help them to empathise with learners, while also enhancing their confidence as teachers through the development and extension of their skills in different contexts.

Team processes

It is appropriate to stress the role that teams can play in supporting both individual and organisational learning, and to emphasise that one of the defining characteristics of a team is that it is a group which is learning how to learn. Senge (1990) argues that 'team learning has three critical dimensions':

First, there is the need to think insightfully about complex issues. Here, teams must learn how to tap the potential for many minds to be more intelligent than one mind.

Second, there is a need for innovative co-ordinated action ... outstanding teams (develop) an 'operational trust'.

Third ... a learning team continually fosters other learning teams. (pp. 236–7)

Senge goes on to discuss the importance of team learning as a 'collective discipline' and of the importance of 'dialogue and discussion'. In these respects team learning is a macrocosm of organisational learning.

Team processes can enhance individual learning when team tasks such as meetings, projects, etc. are managed so as to emphasise the importance of planning and review and to stress the role of the team leader as coach. Teams can provide secure environments in which to make mistakes, opportunities for 'apprentices' to complete projects in a 'no risk' environment. Most importantly, because the mature team is able to deploy sophisticated interpersonal relationships, creativity and the achievement of understanding are facilitated.

In some ways the whole problem of the identification of techniques and strategies to support professional learning would be significantly ameliorated if all schools, staff and pupils were able to work and learn in genuine teams.

5

■ ■ ■

Identifying and Diagnosing Needs

This chapter is essentially about the appraisal of teachers although it has to be stressed from the outset that the principles and practices explored have to be applicable to every adult in the school if a learning organisation is to be created. The use of the term appraisal is surrounded with confusion and its semantics are fraught with multiple interpretations. The chapter will therefore deal with three broad themes: first, appraisal as it is required by law; second, needs analysis in the context of the learning organisation; and finally the issue of poor performance.

One of the major problems surrounding the introduction of legally and contractually binding appraisal was the multiplicity of functions it had to serve. At the heart of the problem was the notion of accountability – appraisal was intended to be developmental but attempts were made to relate it to pay and career development, and its relationship to disciplinary procedures and sanctions was ambivalent. In the final analysis this ambiguity resulted in the Appraisal Regulations being modified, compromised and finally ignored in many schools. If professional learning is to become axiomatic to a teacher's working life then there have to be organisational processes to support it. However, the deficit model for most organisations, hierarchy and bureaucratic control, means that it is very difficult to reconcile learning with organisational efficiency.

A model that helps to clarify and elucidate the tensions of this situation can be found in the concept of mature and immature organisations. In essence, just as with individuals making the transition from immaturity to maturity, so organisations go through stages in which the relationship between control and trust gradually changes. A young teenager will be given a specific time to be in at night and sanctions will be applied if they are late. As trust increases so controls and sanctions are lifted. One of the main problems for the education

IMMATURE	MATURE
CONTROL	TRUST
Structures	Relationships
Teaching	Learning
Bureaucracy	Values
Inspection	Self-review
Hierarchy	Community
Compliance	Consent
Management	Leadership

Figure 5.1: Immature and mature organisations

system is that it is not trusted and there are many controls and sanctions applied at the national level. However, at the institutional level it is possible to move across the continuum of control to trust in many significant areas. Figure 5.1 illustrates the components of this relationship. The tension between control and trust is the fundamental one and it has to be said straight away that it is much easier, and far less time-consuming, to control rather than to trust. Control implies superordinate relationships with sanctions available and the means of enforcement. Trust, by complete contrast, involves acceptance, a willingness to 'let go'. As Fukuyama (1995) defines it:

Trust is the expectation that arises within a community of regular, honest and co-operative behaviour, based on commonly shared norms, on the part of other members of the community. Those norms can be about 'deep' value questions like the nature of God or justice, but they also encompass secular norms like professional standards and codes of behaviour. (p. 26)

The lack of trust entails 'transaction costs' (Fukuyama, 1995) – the costs of generating and enforcing roles and regulations, controls and sanctions, structures and systems.

Where trust has been created then formal management structures can be replaced by sophisticated relationships. Teaching as the formal transmission of knowledge is replaced by learning as the creation of personal meaning and understanding. The control culture of bureaucratic systems is replaced by consensus derived from explicit and shared values. This in turn allows accountability to be expressed through self-review rather than externally imposed inspection. Formal, hierarchical structures are replaced by a notion of community in which roles and status are redundant and so management to obtain compliance is replaced by leadership based on consent. As Handy (1989) puts it:

Intelligent people prefer to agree rather than to obey. (p. 128)

and

Let us make no mistake: the cultures of consent are not easy to run, or to work in. (p. 132)

The learning organisation is an intelligent organisation and demonstrates its maturity through trust and recognition that it can only improve through the professional learning of all the members of the community.

Most models of appraisal are exemplifications of hierarchical and bureaucratic systems, based as they are on a lack of respect for the capacity of the individual to be responsible for their personal growth and professional learning. One of the most powerful manifestations of the immature organisation is the concept of 'performance management'. In this context 'performance' implies a contrived output – 'jumping through hoops' – and is redolent of the circus. 'Management' is tautologous with control, efficiency and a view of the world as linear and predictable. The learning of individuals is not linear, predictable or controllable (the delivery of the curriculum might be) but is random, chaotic and not subject to the pseudo-rationalism of managerialism.

It may well be that organisations have to go through a process of maturing – moving from the manifestations of immaturity to the complexity and sophistication of a fully mature community. Unfortunately there may be a temptation not to move beyond the immature organisation; it is sometimes easier to manage and be managed rather than to lead and learn. Chapter 2 demonstrated the components of and criteria for a learning organisation. For educational organisations this has to be seen as a goal and any other organisational form as essentially transitional.

The next section considers teacher appraisal as required in England and Wales as a starting point for moving from a simplistic view of managing staff development to a more sophisticated model of professional learning.

Teacher appraisal

The history of schoolteacher appraisal in England and Wales is fraught with ambiguity and controversy. The developments that took place in the 1980s eventually produced a consensus that appeared to be capable of implementation but for the lack of funding. The report of the Advisory Conciliation and Arbitration Service (ACAS) Independent Panel (1986) defined teacher appraisal as:

a continuous and systematic process intended to help individual teachers with their professional development and career planning, and to help ensure that the in-service training and deployment of teachers matches the complementary needs of individual teachers and the schools. (para. 3)

This view was largely implemented through the Education (School Teacher Appraisal) Regulations 1991 and Circular 12/91. These two documents remain the basis of the legal and contractual status of appraisal although it is doubtful if there are many LEAs or schools observing the letter of the law.

The essential features of appraisal under the Regulations are as follows:

Aims

To improve the quality of education for pupils by

- recognising the achievements of teachers and enhancing their performance;
- managing the deployment of teachers;
- linking career development to in-service training;
- supporting teachers through guidance and counselling;
- providing data for references;
- improving the management of schools.

Scope

All qualified teachers employed on full-time permanent contracts. Every aspect of a teacher's work might be appraised.

Who appraises?

The headteacher nominates a teacher's appraiser, who would normally have management responsibility for the work of the teacher. Headteachers and teachers should not normally choose their appraisers.

The appraisal cycle

A continuous two-year cycle throughout a teacher's career:
Year 1
- An initial planning meeting
- Self-appraisal (optional)
- Classroom observation (compulsory)
- A review and target-setting interview.

Year 2
- A review meeting to monitor progress.

Management

Appraisal records to be kept – copies of targets to be passed to the INSET co-ordinator, otherwise confidential. The guidance notes indicate that appraisal should be carried out in the context of the school development plan and the targets should be integrated into a whole school. A clear distinction has to be drawn between the appraisal process and any other management process, e.g. promotion, selection, capability or grievance.

A significant number of factors conspired to limit the implementation of this approach to appraisal:

- the lack of additional resources to meet the demands, especially in terms of time, on schools and teachers;
- continuing uncertainty about the confidentiality of the process and the uses to which appraisal might be put (a semantic confusion between appraisal and assessment remains endemic);
- lack of confidence in the competence and capability of appraisers;
- the limited infrastructure available to support the meeting of appraisal targets;
- the fact that many schools lacked a fully developed strategy for human resource management into which appraisal could be integrated.

It remains a bizarre fact that schoolteachers are perhaps the only group of employees to be compelled into an appraisal scheme by law. Such a pedigree is hardly auspicious for the success of a scheme focused on development. In spite of this many LEAs and schools have operated highly successful appraisal schemes, usually modifying the Regulations to produce a bespoke and appropriate scheme.

In their large-scale study of the implementation of teacher appraisal in schools Wragg *et al.* (1996) came to the overall conclusion that:

> The principal purpose of appraisal is to improve practice ... daily teaching consists of hundreds and thousands of interactions, many similar to each other. Changing these practices and habits for the better is not easily achieved when they have been laid down firmly and repetitively over many years. Even the very best teachers can still improve what they do, yet it is far easier not to change than to change. (p. 201)

On the basis of this proposition their findings would appear to indicate that the 'official' appraisal scheme operates under profound constraints in terms of principle and practice, e.g.

Almost all teachers set targets, two each on average, but teachers were divided about the effectiveness of these, and a significant minority were unable to recall them at all. (p. 187)

There seemed to be little sophistication in the methods of observation used by appraisers. (p. 188)

After appraisal was over about 70 per cent of teachers said they had derived personal benefits from it, but slightly under half claimed that they had actually changed their classroom practice as a result of being appraised. (p. 188)

There were appraisers who determined the agenda, sometimes quite forcefully, occasionally refusing to give way, perhaps by not being willing to accept the appraisee's choice of focus. In one case the head decided the area of focus for the whole school. (p. 188)

While there would appear to be flaws and problems in almost every aspect of the appraisal process there did seem to be a range of positive aspects. Indeed 69 per cent of teachers in the Wragg *et al.* survey claimed to have derived some personal benefit. This may have been in terms of perceived career development or may simply have been a 'Hawthorne' effect – the opportunity to focus on self and a measure of positive recognition and feedback. But if, as Wragg *et al.* state above, the 'principal purpose of appraisal is to improve practice' then both the design and implementation of the Appraisal Regulations appear profoundly constrained. Not only is the model conceptually limited but it is an exemplification of an approach to management that is itself limited and inappropriate. The need is for a model that can deal with the complexities of improving learning and teaching and be consistent with principles of school improvement and effective leadership.

Needs analysis in the learning organisation

Barth (1990) offers a wonderful parable of the relationship between the formal, bureaucratic approach to managing staff development and a mature approach based on respect for the individual. He describes (pp. 51–2) how he planted an orchard in symmetrical rows apart from two trees which were planted in a corner of the orchard and forgotten. In spite of lavish attention and care the orchard produced little fruit with some trees dying and others diseased. Needless to say the two neglected trees flourished and produced copious amounts of fruit. Barth goes on to draw the following conclusion:

I find that staff development is least effective when planned, premeditated, and deliberate. When principals set out to train teachers, run workshops, conduct inservice training, or direct faculty meetings, I see only modest professional change come to teachers. On the other hand, I find professional development most likely to occur as a consequence of teacher and principal imaginatively pursuing regular school issues and functions together. (p. 59)

Barth is not advocating an abdication of responsibility for professional learning and development but rather their emergence from working collaboratively on matters of shared significance. He goes on to identify three broad categories of teachers in the context of professional learning (pp. 53–4):

1 Teachers who are unable and unwilling to reflect on their own practice and unable to accept the scrutiny of others.
2 Teachers who are able to reflect and change but who are unable to accept the insights and support of others.
3 'A small number' who are able to both reflect and change and involve others in the improvement of their practice.

To Barth's list might be added a fourth category – those who are highly dependent on others but are unable to internalise through reflection and thus exist in a state of subordination. Figure 5.2 shows the relationship between these four positions; reordering them produces the following classification:

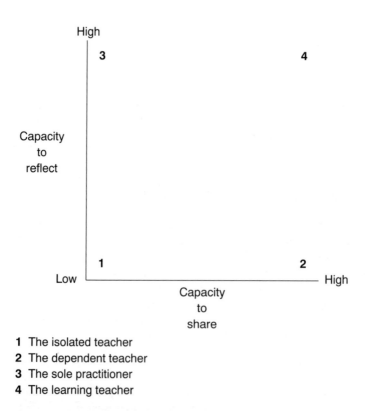

1 The isolated teacher
2 The dependent teacher
3 The sole practitioner
4 The learning teacher

Figure 5.2: Teachers' capacity to learn

1   The dependent teacher – an instrumental approach with limited application, development or learning.

2   The isolated teacher – no reflection, no learning and so no improvement.

3   The sole practitioner – capable of reflection but unable to share and communicate so limiting their potential.

4   The learning teacher – able to reflect on their own work and accept insights from others.

The isolated teacher is going nowhere, working in a purely functional way to get through the lesson, the day, the curriculum; they are often adequately competent but unable to improve and, perhaps crucially, to learn from and support the learning of others. Perhaps the greatest danger of this type of teacher is the culture that exists in their classrooms – individualistic, instrumental and inhibited. The dependent teacher by contrast is all too willing to listen to others – in fact they may be unable to function in the absence of explicit guidelines. Most of us have experienced this in a new job or a new school. As a transitional phase this is a perfectly valid position – the danger is that it becomes institutionalised: 'Tell me what to do and I'll do it.' This teacher may be adequately efficient but their learning will always be shallow and superficial and they will not be able to develop their own praxis – they will always be classroom technicians, never artists.

The sole practitioner may well perceive themselves as the apotheosis of professionalism and there is no doubt that they will embody many of the characteristics of a successful teacher. However, they will probably ignore whole-school issues and be reluctant to incorporate available best practice into their own work – even though they might discover it in time. They may well be the embodiment of the 'limited professional' – excellent in their own domain but will not participate in school-wide improvement strategies. There is also the problem that with a limited range of sources for their reflection that reflection will become increasingly constrained and self-legitimating.

The major problem with the learning teacher is likely to be exhaustion. Barth (1990) characterises them thus:

> ... able and willing to critically scrutinise their practice and are quite able and willing, even desirous, of making their practice accessible to other adults ... They seek us out, tend to be the most able, and make us feel the most comfortable and successful, although they probably need us the least. (p. 54)

The learning teacher is also to be cherished because they exemplify what most schools aspire to for their pupils – they are the most powerful of role models and in ideal circumstances are probably known as leaders of classrooms, teams and schools.

Clearly the issue for professional learning is to help colleagues in the first three categories to move towards the fourth. To achieve this requires a sophisticated balance of techniques applied within a supportive culture. This is the essence of needs analysis – help in reflection and sharing against public and agreed criteria. In the context of professional learning needs analysis has to be as personal a process as learning is itself. The tension between individual and organisational imperatives is resolved not by the forced cultivation of an orchard but by encouraging growth in idiosyncratic ways to achieve a common purpose. In her discussion of effective leadership Wheatley (1992) draws parallels between the scientific principles of chaos and complexity – the 'odd combination of predictability and self-determination' (p. 133) – and working in organisations and she stresses:

> ... the importance of simple governing principles: guiding visions, strong values, organisational beliefs – the few roles individuals can use to shape their own behaviour. The leader's task is to communicate them, to keep them ever-present and clear, and then allow individuals in the system their random, sometimes chaotic looking meanderings. (p. 133)

Barth's delight in his two trees that produced a wonderful crop of apples would have been very different if they had produced plums. They grew idiosyncratically but they produced apples – this is the balance between the individual and the greater purpose. It is a primary purpose of leadership to create the meaning that sets the context for professional learning.

In its most basic form the issue of needs analysis can be reduced to three simple questions:

1 Where do I need to be?
2 Where am I now?
3 How do I move from 2 to 1?

If the answer to the first question is seen as a destination then it is one of the key functions of leadership to create meaning – to make the destination understood and to achieve acceptance of its validity. The greater the understanding and acceptance the more likely it is that there will be a rich crop of apples. The clarity of the destination also helps to define the starting point and to identify the most appropriate means of travelling.

Defining the destination

Figure 5.3 shows the components of organisational outcomes which have to be in place to contextualise professional learning. Unless these are in place and explicit then ambiguity will almost inevitably result in a loss of effectiveness and the wasting of scarce resources in redefining and articulating anew.

The various components of the context may be defined as follows:

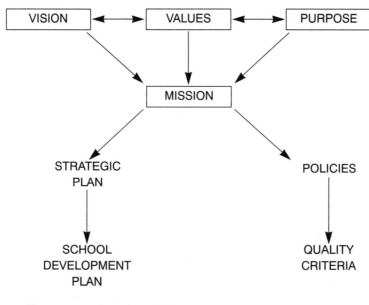

Figure 5.3: The context of needs analysis

- **Vision:** a description of the school as it should be and needs to be in the future. Using techniques such as futures thinking the school draws a picture of itself in 10–15 years, time, taking into account discernible trends such as the growth of IT, and definitions of fundamental processes such as learning and social relationships. The vision thus attempts to reconcile trends that will impact on the school with beliefs about the nature of education.

- **Values:** explicit statements about the ethical and moral basis on which the school will operate. These relate to such issues as the status of the individual, the basis for decision making, relationships with the community, codes of conduct and the nature of the school as a moral community.

- **Purpose:** many organisations, including schools, are unclear as to their core purpose. Is it to teach the National Curriculum, to create autonomous learners or to provide a safe and caring environment? It may be all three but a school needs to be aware of what it is actually trying to achieve.

- **Mission:** an increasing number of schools now have mission statements. At their best they have the following characteristics:
  - they are the result of a collaborative process;
  - they are understood and accepted by all members of the school community;
  - they feature prominently in all aspects of school life;
  - they are used as the fundamental benchmark for all decisions.
  The effective and meaningful mission statement is a distillation of the school's vision, values and purpose.

97

- **Strategic plan:** this renders the mission statement into a three- to five-year plan, translating principles and aspirations into specific outcomes and recognising the staffing and resource implications.
- **School development plan:** this in turn translates the strategic plan into shorter-term (12–18 months) targets which are more specific and allow team and individual target setting.
- **Policies:** are the exemplification of the mission statement into specific areas of the school's activity so as to provide guidelines to inform collective and individual behaviour.
- **Quality criteria:** these are the specific criteria which serve as definitions of effectiveness in the many different circumstances of school life. Job descriptions and codes of conduct are common examples; however, quality criteria are written in terms of outcomes – what should be the result rather than a simple description of the process.

These various components can be exemplified in respect of pupils' learning:

- **Vision:** a school in which pupils are helped to take increasing responsibility for their own learning and standards of achievement are consistently raised.
- **Values:** a focus on the individual and the integrity of their experience as a learner.
- **Purpose:** to produce confident, autonomous learners.
- **Mission:** XYZ school is a learning community which respects the right of every individual to learn and achieve in a caring and supportive environment.
- **Strategic plan:** to move towards individualisation of the curriculum over five years.
- **School development plan:** to enhance the use of IT to facilitate individual learning programmes.
- **Policies:** a learning policy which sets out the school's philosophy of learning.
- **Quality criteria:** definitions of the most propitious circumstances for learning in a variety of contexts.

The professional learning of the individual teacher is thus contextualised but not circumscribed. It is worth stressing that the development of these various components is, in itself, a major learning process. If plans and policies are to work they have to be based on consent and derived from a sophisticated process of shared perception and formulation.

Apart from what the school exists to do there are two other broad categories which individual learners need to relate to in order to understand their learning needs. First there is what might be called the 'canon' of professional knowledge – writings about principles, descriptions of alternative modes of practice and the results of research into educational matters, the focus of the concerns of teachers as intellectuals which may serve to challenge, to confirm or result in denial. Increasingly such ideas may be drawn from outside a purely educational canon, e.g. the neurological basis of learning, the concept of the learning organisation, the notion of community.

The third element is professional practice – the accumulated wisdom and experience of others, tried and tested over time and validated by success. This practice might be as complex as working with children with profound learning difficulties or as basic as managing a meeting. In both cases understanding another person's successful practice can be a major source of insight, challenge, confirmation or denial.

The relative significance of each of these three will vary according to individual and organisational need. For example, a decision to radically redesign a school's literacy strategy will probably need to go outside habitual practice in order to generate new ideas and their related practices. Concern about standards in A level English teaching may be resolved by reference to strategies used in another sixth form or in the history department of the same school. Sometimes an external stimulus is essential; on other occasions internal consolidation is most appropriate.

The three elements taken together constitute the map of professional effectiveness – the answer to the question 'How do I know what I need to know?'

Starting points

Nothing is more important than knowing the starting point of a journey in relation to the destination – it determines both the direction and pace of travel. Needs analysis provides the crucial information to ensure that professional learning is appropriate, valid and relevant. A variety of techniques are available all of which are essentially concerned with diagnosis on the basis of evidence in order to inform perceptions and so determine action. Evidence is the essential component of this process. Such evidence can be obtained in a number of ways; significantly most of these have already been noted in Chapter 4. The common element is feedback – from a coach or mentor, through a diagnostic review or as the result of a survey. Evidence is also available in terms of the results or outcomes of a particular part of the curriculum or course. In almost every case the validity and reliability of such evidence is open to question – if only because of the range of variables that have to be taken into account in forming a judgement.

Central to the Appraisal Regulations and to most review schemes is the notion of observation of classroom or management practice. In its simplest form classroom observation comprises an initial meeting to set up a protocol for the observation, the observation itself and some form of feedback. Even this simplistic model appears fraught with difficulties. Wragg and his colleagues (1996) report that 40 per cent chose an aspect of management for their focus with class management and teaching methods second and third. Over half the observations reported in the survey lasted for less than 45 minutes. Most teachers received some form of feedback within 48 hours. As far as the actual experience is concerned:

> ... *primary teachers reported being more affected by, and less happy at the presence of an observer, than secondary teachers. Female teachers were more affected and less happy than male teachers ... Male teachers who had male appraisers were distinctly more happy at being observed ... (p. 85)*

Quite irrespective of the valuable findings of this survey and the issues arising from the management of aspects of the scheme is the overall conclusion of Wragg *et al.*:

> *The major impact of appraisal seems to have been more on beliefs, attitudes and relationships than on action, and this should give considerable food for thought. (p. 185)*

This substantial reservation has to be reinforced by a questioning of the fundamental integrity of the observation process as a precursor to professional learning. Although the majority of teachers accepted the observation, consider the following factors:

1   Most appraisers held management positions that were superior to the appraisee.
2   Most observations were of one, short, negotiated lesson.
3   There was abundant notice of the observation – the possibility of a 'special' lesson was very real. ('I really enjoyed that lesson, Sir. Were you being appraised?')
4   The stakes were relatively low, the significance of the observation was limited.
5   The whole process occupied a very small amount of time and was not integrated into the full range of school management activities.

Not all of these factors are necessarily negative but they do combine to create a sense of dislocation and artificiality. To these specific concerns have to be added a number of broader conceptual issues:

1   The very process of observation places the observed in a subordinate role. There is an inevitable power relationship which diminishes the observed.
2   The observer inevitably compromises the integrity of the lesson. It is naive to pretend that the presence of a non-participant will not distort the integrity of what is being observed.
3   The integrity of the observation will also be a function of the integrity of the data recording process. Wragg and his colleagues found that the majority of observers recorded their observations in a freehand non-structured way. The validity and reliability of such data is highly questionable.

4 Drawing conclusions from such data is also very problematic. The interpretation and analysis of any activity is subject to a wide range of variables not the least of which are the competing value systems of observer and observed.

Underlying these points is the issue of a claim to objectivity and the consequent belief that future behaviour can be predicted on the basis of responses to the observation. This is confirmed by the limited impact on teacher behaviour described by *Wragg et al.* and discussed above.

If teachers are to understand how they are functioning in classrooms and in their leadership and management roles then there has to be a more effective way of gathering valid data to inform needs analysis. The most appropriate strategies are those identified in Chapters 3 and 4 – reflection and coaching. It is the detailed and systematic review in the context of a long-term relationship that will generate data to inform learning.

Specific strategies that will generate valid data which is not compromised by status, randomness or subjectivity are:

- **Coaching:** a long-term non-hierarchical relationship which combines diagnosis, analysis and strategies for action. The long-term relationship facilitates the development of trust and so openness and acceptance. The key contribution of the coach is to facilitate detailed understanding of actual processes and then to be involved in any developmental strategies agreed.

- **Critical friendship:** this is also known as a teaching partnership. What distinguishes it from coaching is that it is a peer and reciprocal relationship but again it is ongoing and the relationship subsumes the analysis and meeting of needs. Although sensitive and empathic coaching is vital in a number of developmental contexts, working directly with colleagues is also very powerful:

   Teachers who interact with their peers learn and practice many of the interpersonal skills and develop the repertoire of tactics ... This informal learning situation can present them with the opportunity ... to develop a capacity for empathy ... to acquire a sensitivity to knowing which lines of action are most appropriate ... and to become more skilled at employing the interpersonal skills needed to develop a mutual definition of the situation that facilitates one teacher's ability to influence another. (Blumberg, 1980, p. 231)

However, as Alfonso and Goldsberry (1982) point out:

   Colleagueship among teachers is typically ignored and often inhibited by the school's formal organisation; consequently, teachers are frequently isolated from their colleagues. This isolation ... drastically impedes the professional development of even the most conscientious and dedicated teachers. (p. 106)

The advantages of such colleagueship or critical friendship is stressed by Little (1982) who found that sustained professional learning was most likely to occur when:

> *. . . teachers engage in frequent, continuous, and increasingly concrete and precise talk about teaching practice . . . By such talk, teachers build up a shared language adequate to the complexity of teaching, capable of distinguishing one practice and its virtues from another, and capable of integrating large bodies of practice into distinct and sensible perspectives on the business of teaching . . . (p. 331).*

It is the mutuality of experience and language that is the most powerful antidote to the artificiality of classroom observation and the dislocated involvement with an appraiser.

Of course the biggest barriers to a critical friendship approach are fundamental to the design of most schools – the isolation of classrooms and the dominance of timetables. However, if the imperative of one teacher, one period, one class can be broken then the potential is enormous – and the potential benefit for pupils is also enormous.

- **Teachers as researchers:** this is perhaps the most powerful, valid and appropriate means of diagnosis and needs analysis. Smyth (1995, p. 106) proposes four key questions fundamental to critical pedagogy:
  - describing . . . what do I do?
  - informing . . . what does this mean?
  - confronting . . . how did I come to be like this?
  - reconstructing . . . how might I do things differently?

Fundamental to these questions is the notion of the teacher as researcher. The extent to which learning, growth and improvement takes place is directly proportionate to the quality of the data that is available to answer Smyth's questions. The more accurate, complete and detailed the answers, the more likely is a strategy that will work. As was argued in Chapter 4, the structures and disciplines of formal research may not always be appropriate to the analysis of classroom and professional practice. However, awareness of such principles and their incorporation into the model of action research described in Chapter 4 does occur in some schools. Douglas (1991) describes the approach adopted at Branston School and Community College in Lincolnshire.

> *The key feature of the Branston proposal . . . is that teachers themselves can be active in promoting changes of style or content which will lead to significant developments across the curriculum . . .*
>
> *. . . projects should be collaborative. Participation in them, the process, should be regarded as an important outcome in itself, as a way of supporting the view that school self-analysis and self-renewal are key aspects of a teacher's professionality . . .*
>
> *The simulation of direct consideration of, or research into, what happens at the point of learning should be an aim.*
>
> *Are you tired of being told by 'experts' what teaching and learning is like? Wouldn't you be the best placed, most fully aware, most professionally skilled*

person to find out – by noticing, or designing situations, or collecting statistics or timing happenings, or interviewing, or tape-recording, or filming or mutual observation or, . . . or . . . (pp. 89–90).

The 'Branston approach' focused resources and activity within the school and its success is demonstrated in the following:

Considering that over one-third of the teachers at Branston have been involved in school based work in each of the last three years the level of disruption has been very low. (p. 89)

When I look at the curriculum map of one term of the third year that the curriculum of learning group has produced, I can see behind its apparent simplicity to the potentially transforming processes that went into it . . . (p. 107).

This discussion has sought to show that needs analysis has to be driven by the teacher within an agreed context of school improvement and has to be a constituent element of the learning process. The use of bureaucratic and hierarchical methods creates high levels of artificiality and dislocates the learning process by reinforcing dependency and removing it from the natural rhythm of personal review, analysis and action. The Appraisal Regulations, in particular, make professional development an arbitrary and potentially dysfunctional activity divorced from teachers' actual experience.

The incompetent teacher

Most of what has been written so far in this chapter and indeed this book does not apply to some teachers. Ignoring the debate about how many teachers are actually technically incompetent the fact remains that there are some who, for a variety of reasons, are unable to work to an acceptable standard – whatever that might be. It is salutary to remind ourselves at this stage that every teacher deemed incompetent was once appointed and presumably satisfied the selection panel that they were the person who met the person and role specification.

A second issue is that a person may be perceived as being incompetent when in fact they have no knowledge as to what constitutes competence. If a role is not appropriately defined, if there are no criteria available which specify appropriate levels of performance, then it is possible that leaders and managers are at least partially responsible. This might be defined as innocent or naive incompetence, a lack of awareness of what is required and an inability to find out. A related phenomenon is the lack of knowledge, skills or capability which is not the result of a malicious or malevolent attitude but, again, the result of innocence.

If these factors are isolated together with aspects of poor performance related to physical and psychological health and disciplinary matters then the issue is clearly one of the willingness of the individual to develop. The dilemma of managing poor performance is demonstrated in Figure 5.4.

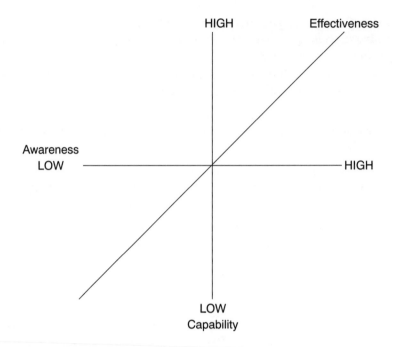

Figure 5.4: Understanding teacher effectiveness

In this model awareness is the understanding that a teacher has of her or his own situation – the extent to which they are sensitive to the context in which they function. Capability is the level of knowledge, skills and experience that can be deployed to meet the needs of a particular task. The combination of high levels of awareness and capability result in effectiveness, i.e. knowing what has to be done and being able to do it. The permutations of the various elements in Figure 5.4 can be explained thus:

Awareness	**Capability**	
LOW	LOW	Classically incompetent, unaware of personal performance and unaware of the lack of skills.
HIGH	LOW	The novice who knows what needs to be done and is willing to learn.
LOW	HIGH	Possesses the skills but may not be developing them or using them to best effect.
HIGH	HIGH	The teacher as learner – the problem is to sustain them.

The first three categories are all areas where optimum effectiveness is compromised. Raising capability is relatively simple assuming that there is an acceptance, an awareness, of the need to raise that capability. Strategies to heighten that awareness could include:

1 Creating an understanding of what is required, e.g. ensuring that the individual is fully aware of all the elements in Figure 5? This is the classic function of leadership – communicating to ensure understanding and to create shared meaning. This is also a team responsibility – to help every team member achieve 'alignment' of values, purpose and outcomes.

2 Setting performance standards on the basis of quality criteria and target setting. The role of the coach is to ensure understanding of what is required in terms of specific performance. The National Commission for Education (1996) found that successful schools 'left very little to chance':

> Each of the successful schools endeavours to have a unified approach to the aims of the school. This often requires an explicit agreement among teachers about their aims and the implementation of policies and systems ... (p. 318).

Most teachers will recognise the fact that the most successful teachers are those who work on explicit and understood requirements in terms of behaviour, standards of work, etc. Ambiguity is not conducive to improvement.

3 In some instances challenge and confrontation may be appropriate – not in the sense of aggression or indignation but rather in a directive, counselling model. This requires a high degree of skill in conflict management and negotiating strategies if it is not to degenerate into the abusive exchange of perceptions. The chances are such an approach will almost invariably reveal some personal situation which has compromised motivation and so the awareness of poor performance.

4 The use of appropriate role-models can provide insights if carefully chosen. The individual with low awareness has to be helped to understand where they are – to do this requires exemplars of how they need to be. Shadowing, paired observation and the opportunity to discover alternative, often better, ways can create the necessary shift.

In the final analysis the awareness of a colleague is a complex and sensitive process involving self-esteem, motivation and a high degree of emotional significance. One of the key characteristics of effective leaders is their capacity to work in this domain.

Conclusion

This chapter has argued that the process of needs analysis in the context of professional learning is not served by bureaucratic and hierarchical systems.

Needs analysis has to be implicit to the learning process and has to grow out of the perceptions of the individual. For this reason it has to be rooted in coaching and reflection and draw on data which is significant and meaningful to the individual. How needs, once identified, are managed is discussed in the next chapter.

6

■ ■ ■

Leading and Managing School-Based Development

The purpose of this chapter is to examine the practical implications for school management of the principles established in the preceding chapters. We are very conscious of many examples of excellent practice in schools and have drawn on a range of generic examples to illuminate this discussion. We are equally aware of an enormous range of practice, some highly innovative and consistent with the principles we have identified, some valid according to different criteria and some marginal to the school and of limited impact. One of the central concerns about the role and status of professional learning is the uncertainty and inconsistency of practice. This chapter offers strategies to help make it central to school management and implicit to every process. Most importantly is to see professional learning as a distinguishing feature of leadership functions.

Many of the structures, policies and approaches described in this chapter are derived from a simple maxim – to change perceptions and behaviour one has first to change language and expectations. The creation of a new vocabulary is an essential precursor to the changing of culture. All teachers know that classes of children will respond differently to teachers, and one of the key factors is the classroom culture that is created through language, consistent behaviour and reinforcement of appropriate responses. If professional learning is to take place in the context of the school as a learning community then there has to be a shared understanding created through the consistent usage of an appropriate vocabulary which informs practice. All schools have the essential structures in place – what is sometimes lacking is the definition of professional learning.

Figure 6.1 demonstrates the relationship between the various structural elements necessary to make the transition from marginalised INSET to integrated professional learning – these will be explored in the text relevant to each component.

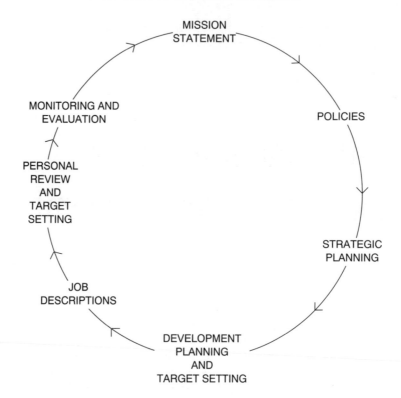

Figure 6.1: School strategies to support professional learning

The status and relationship of each component can be explained as follows:

- **Mission statement:** the overarching statement of the nature and purpose of the school which acts as the basis for all policy making.
- **Policies:** statements which articulate specific components of the mission statement relevant to the full range of the school's activities.
- **Strategic planning:** translation of the policies into long-term (5–10 years) intentions.
- **Development planning and target setting:** translation of the strategic plan into specific short-term (12–18 months) outcomes and relating these to the budgetary process.
- **Job descriptions:** unique and individual statements which indicate the specific contribution of each individual to the school's mission, policies and plans.
- **Personal review and target setting:** translating the school's short-term objectives into personal action plans and identifying personal and generic learning outcomes.

- **Monitoring and evaluation:** strategies for ensuring that intentions are being translated into practice and contributing to the overall achievement of the school's mission.

Creating structures to support professional learning

Figure 6.1 is expressed as a circular diagram to reinforce the notion that organisational learning is a cyclical process and as each cycle is completed so the school moves on – modifying its mission, adjusting its policies to meet changing needs and circumstances. In theory at least the developmental circle matures into an upward spiral as the school learns, modifies and improves. In this sense it is possible to see the school as a macrocosm of individual, personalised learning. The issue is to identify simple, facilitative structures which do not become ends in themselves but are rather vehicles for learning and are only valid and significant to the extent to which they facilitate individual learning in an organisational context. The great danger with the model described in Figure 6.1 is that it takes on a life of its own and serves as the basis for bureaucratic management rather than supporting leadership and learning.

In order to avoid the danger of bureaucratisation and the dominance of organisational management over individual learning and leadership the various components described in Figure 6.1 may have to be reconstituted using an appropriate vocabulary. The following sections explore how each of the components identified above can be aligned with the notion of professional learning and leadership. In most cases the changes are semantic – but it is through language that meaning is created.

The mission statement

A mission statement is essentially the promises that a school makes to its pupils, staff and the wider community. In its most basic manifestation, school leadership exists to keep those promises. It is therefore essential that the right promises are made. Every school has a mission statement or a set of aims (it really doesn't matter which). What is often not the case is that the mission statement is appropriately formulated and that it plays a central role in school leadership and management.

In the context of the school as a learning organisation and with an emphasis on professional learning the mission statement might include a component such as:

- Our primary purpose is to create a learning community in which everyone can develop their intellectual, social, moral and spiritual potential.

A more specific statement might take the following form:

- We will recognise learning as an individual process and design school structures and processes to support individual achievement.

Both of these statements are explicit about the centrality of learning and make a clear and unambiguous promise as to the school's commitment. The other important point about both of these promises is that they are equally applicable to the smallest primary school and the largest secondary school; they are valid for the inner-city school and the most Arcadian of suburban schools. The statements are explicit about learning, the core purpose of any school, and about the integrity of the individual, pupil or member of staff, and are focused on potential and achievement.

However, such statements mean nothing if they are not integrated into every aspect of the school's life. The status of the mission statement will be enhanced if it is:

- regularly placed on the agenda of all meetings;
- used as the basis for assemblies and social and personal development sessions;
- made part of the criteria for the promotion and selection of staff;
- integrated into the budgetary cycle as a means of prioritising the allocation of scarce resources;
- used as part of the criteria for the employment of trainers and consultants;
- directly integrated into the formulation of policies and plans.

It is this latter point that is perhaps pivotal – the purpose of policies and planning is to translate the moral intent and professional aspirations of the mission statement into the actual experience of each member of the school community.

Policies

Schools have to have a wide range of policies – some claim to have in excess of 50 – covering every aspect of the life of the school. It would be tedious to list even a few as exemplifications but what is significant is the fact that comparatively few schools have an explicit policy relating to learning. A policy on learning should include the following elements:

1 A definition of learning, e.g. 'Learning is a unique and subjective process which results in understanding, internalisation and the capacity to act autonomously. A distinction is drawn between shallow learning – memorisation and replication – and profound learning which is expressed through personal change.'

2 A definition of the role of the teacher in the learning process, i.e. specifying

the nature of coaching, the relationship between teacher and learner and the responsibility of the teacher to be a learner.

3 Recognition of the range of teaching strategies and their relationship to effective learning.

4 Definition of the relationship between learning and assessment and the specification of appropriate assessment strategies.

5 Identification of the nature and purpose of pastoral care and its relationship to learning, in particular strategies for raising achievement.

6 An indication of the provision of resources and the basis of access to them.

7 A reinforcement and specific application of the school's equal opportunities policy with particular regard to the entitlement to effective learning.

8 A recognition of the contribution of wider learning opportunities, e.g. the home, community, etc.

One of the defining characteristics of such a policy is that for most purposes it should refer to all members of the school community on equal terms and should not differentiate between pupils, staff and (most invidiously) 'non-teaching' or 'support' staff.

To work such a policy has to be central to every relevant activity and at the heart of syllabuses, lesson planning as well as professional learning activities. The policy can also serve as an explicit criterion in discussions about effectiveness and the selection of development activities.

Strategic planning

At the heart of the strategic planning process in a school should be a long-term strategy to ensure that the promises in the mission statement are kept – most significantly the enhancement of individual learning. The strategic issues that might be included in such a context would be concerned with *inter alia*:

1 The extension of the use of IT as a tool for learning, e.g. the development of a costed programme to increase access to and usage of personal and network computers, extending the use of integrated learning systems and the use of the Internet.

2 Revising the staffing structure of the school to release more time and money to allow for individualised learning strategies.

3 Changes to the pattern of the school day to make more effective usage of limited resources and to recognise the variety of learning patterns that exist.

All of these examples are directly consistent with the mission statement and the policy on learning. What they do is to help prioritise, set a whole-school development agenda and demonstrate a commitment to translating principle into practice.

Development planning and target setting

Once the strategic plan has set priorities then it has to be translated into specific, short-term outcomes which are integrated with the school's budgetary cycle. The principles of school development planning are now well established and understood. However, many do not have learning as an explicit focus. The increasing use of whole-school target setting (underpinned by personal target setting for pupils and staff) provides an opportunity to move the SDP into a focus on the school's core purpose and to create a culture focused on achievement. Examples of short-term targets might include:

- To extend student coaching into years 9 and 10 by September 1998.
- To introduce successmaker into years 5 and 6 by January 1999.
- Through the use of intensive supported reading development strategies to reduce the number of pupils with a reading age two years behind chronological age by 50 per cent within 18 months.
- To introduce the CASE approach (Cognitive Acceleration for Science Education) into year 8 to support the achievement of 60 per cent grade A–C by 2001.

These targets are all examples of proven strategies based on the learning of the individual which can contribute to success. They all have direct implications for the learning and development of teachers and these should also be expressed as targets. They will also need to be whole-school targets relating to the development of teachers, e.g.

- To ensure that by September 1999 all staff are able to word-process, use spreadsheets and databases and access the Internet with confidence.

Targets are undoubtedly useful in helping to sustain a focus and provide a structure; however, they will always be subject to compromise. Individual and organisational learning is not amenable to the imposition of arbitrary targets, they will always be subject to modification. But as a basis for supporting implementation they are a powerful and tested strategy. Earley (1997, p. 45) provides a set of criteria for effective target setting:

- Targets need to be an integral part of school development and improvement plans.
- The likelihood of success is greatest when those responsible for the achievement of targets are involved in setting them.
- Target setting stems from self-evaluation and analysis of practice . . .
- Benchmarking data enable fair comparisons to be made . . .
- The principle of 'improve on previous best' . . . can be a powerful motivator.
- The emphasis should be on measurable *pupil* outcomes.
- Ensure that pupil outcomes other than academic achievement (e.g. attitudes, values, self-esteem) are also considered.

Job description

The concept of the job description is highly problematic and a key characteristic of the immature organisation – especially when it comprises a list of tasks. A detailed, task focused, job description is at best a sign of limited trust and at worst an exemplification of a control culture. But at the same time there is nothing worse than the sense of personal and organisational ambiguity that results from a lack of definition and clarification of priorities. What is clear is that the most professionally appropriate job descriptions are a means of helping the individual relate herself or himself to organisational principles and priorities. It may even be helpful to conceptualise the job description as a form of personal mission statement which is tailored to suit an individual in a specific context and so indicates priorities but is also expressed in such a way as to enhance personal autonomy and the capacity to act.

The job description is also a means of personalising the language of the school's values and its priorities so as to reinforce their applicability in any given context.

Creating a job description is a matter of reconciling the personal and the organisational. Each job description should be unique but it may well contain some generic statements. Examples of such statements might include:

- To provide leadership for the school in order to facilitate the learning of all members of the school community.
- To lead the subject team so as to implement the school's learning policy and raise pupil achievement.
- To offer professional leadership and support the development of colleagues by facilitating self-review and providing coaching and mentoring.
- To provide leadership in the classroom in order to enhance the learning of every individual and so raise achievement.

There is always the danger that this type of statement will appear to be a professional platitude. It will be, unless job descriptions of this type are used as the basis for self-review, the design of professional learning activities and the implementation of leadership practice throughout the school.

The final two elements of Figure 6.1 – *personal review* and *'monitoring and evaluation'* are dealt with in detail in Chapters 5 and 7 respectively and it is not intended to replicate the discussion here.

Strategies to support professional learning

Once an infrastructure which focuses on learning has been created, it then becomes necessary to identify a range of strategies which reinforce and exemplify the principles of organisational and professional learning. What is important is that the processes themselves are seen as significant as well as the outcomes they may lead to.

The learning contract

This strategy is widely used in further and higher education and is used in a variety of forms in many schools. Its use in professional learning is relatively limited. The use of the notion of a 'contract' is sometimes seen as inappropriate because of its formal and legalistic tone. The terminology really doesn't matter – 'learning promise' or 'learning commitment' are just as valid. The important thing is the notion of a reciprocal commitment to engage in a learning process with rights and responsibilities on both sides. The contract is essentially between learner and facilitator; thus it might be between a newly qualified teacher and mentor, two teachers in a learning partnership, a newly appointed headteacher and her or his mentor, a team member and team leader, etc. The learning contract can also be used when a teacher attends an externally provided course, when an external consultant runs a training day or when someone follows an award-bearing programme.

The learning contract will only achieve its full potential if it permeates the whole school and is used in varying guises with pupils. The use of contracts is well known with pupils whose attendance is poor or whose behaviour is inappropriate. It might be appropriate to extend the principle to all pupils to help personalise and individualise their learning. Such a contract would recognise the generic requirements of the curriculum but could be extended to include reference to special needs and personal priorities and to recognise prior learning. Unless learning contracts become the basis for negotiation with pupils about their learning it is doubtful if they will assume the status and significance necessary to become part of professional learning and so fundamental to the creation of a learning culture.

The principles informing the design of a learning contract are the same for headteacher, teacher and pupil and can be expressed in a number of simple questions:

- Why are you engaging in this activity?
- What outcomes are you working towards?
- What do you already know about this area?
- What learning strategies will you use?
- What resources will you need?
- How can your coach/mentor/teacher support you?
- What timescale will you work to?
- How should your learning be assessed?
- How will you know that this project/activity is completed?

These questions might be translated into headings on a pro forma or incorporated into a learning journal. For pupils they could well form a substantial component of a Record of Achievement. For the adults in the school they could be incorporated into a Professional Development Profile. Such profiles are often kept by teachers at the early stages of their careers but often fall into disuse in the later stages. This is a pity as they can be a powerful tool in managing careers, professional learning and development. For a mid-career teacher a profile might include:

- an up-to-date CV
- copies of learning contracts
- details of programmes and courses attended
- job descriptions
- copies of letters of application
- examples of work
- results of diagnostic testing, assessment centres, etc.

The learning contract is a potentially powerful tool to help individuals to focus on their own learning, to take active control of the process and to develop the skills to negotiate personalised learning strategies.

Learning review

This should not be confused with the development review (see below); it is rather a whole-school approach to help create a culture in which everyone is constantly aware of their own learning and that of others. It is a way of moving towards the concept of the learning organisation through simple and specific activities. In essence no activity is completed until all those involved have engaged in a shared and personal review of what has been learnt.

Barber (1997) provides a powerful and lyrical endorsement of this approach:

So in order to help create the learning society what should we ask? Isn't it obvious? The question has to be: 'what did you learn today?' ...

... each time someone asks the question they play a small part in raising the priority society gives to learning, in pushing education up the cultural agenda, in building the social and political momentum, which will assist in the creation of a learning society. (p. 304)

Examples of how this simple but profound question can be used in schools include:

1 Ending every lesson and every day with a few minutes' reflection: 'What did we learn and how did we learn it?' This works with five year olds and headteachers. With the former it increases the possibility of a detailed and positive response to the often asked question 'what did you do in school

today?' It might also help the latter group! It is difficult to imagine a more powerful end to a day in school than teachers and pupils reflecting together, drawing conclusions and recording them in learning journals.

2 Putting review on the agenda of every meeting. Thus agendas do not end with 'Any Other Business' or 'Date of Next Meeting' (examples of bad practice anyway) but with five minutes spent discussing the answers to questions such as: What went well in this meeting? Was everyone able to contribute? Did we achieve appropriate outcomes? How did we manage our time? How can we reinforce and replicate our success?

Thus the final entry in the action plan to emerge from the meeting is a synthesis of good practice.

3 Ending all but the most informal of interviews or discussions with a brief review. At first this might appear artificial but it can rapidly become a norm and is in many ways a profound indication of genuineness and seriousness by seeking feedback on how we worked together as well as what we did.

4 Ensuring that all professional learning activities end with a focus on what has been learnt rather than a comment on the social and domestic arrangements.

This approach to learning review helps to create a culture of significance for learning, gives status to the learning process and creates shared expectations and a common vocabulary. There are few activities more professionally challenging than creating a culture of learning. The deliberate and systematic introduction of shared review is a very tangible step that can be taken at no cost. It will also reinforce what undoubtedly already exists in many classrooms, teams and relationships. It is symbolic of the movement away from managing a lesson or meeting to leading learning.

Developmental review

This is the diagnostic process essential to any professional learning strategy. In many contexts it will already exist in the form of appraisal and there are many significant parallels between the intentions of the Appraisal Regulations and review for professional learning. However, the review process needs to be sharply differentiated from certain aspects of appraisal – essentially its use as part of an accountability model.

The most unsatisfactory aspects of teacher appraisal as far as developmental review is concerned are:

- the use of line-managers as appraisers;
- the artificial and arbitrary requirement for classroom observation;
- the totally artificial timescale, i.e. spreading the process over two years.

Developmental review needs to grow out of and be implicit in a long-term relationship in which diagnosis and action are habitual. The principles for such a review process can be expressed as:

- a long-term relationship, probably involving the coach or mentor;
- regular interactions which are part of the normal pattern of working life;
- formal meetings to review professional effectiveness in the context of the structures described in the first half of this chapter;
- data collection based on the sharing of perceptions, gathering of evidence (perhaps involving observation);
- the setting of agreed targets which reconcile individual and organisational needs;
- coaching and support in order to achieve the targets, especially in the application of skills and knowledge;
- regular opportunities for review and reflection in order to monitor progress, adjust outcomes and modify or revise targets;
- consolidation of success as appropriate and the identification of further targets to sustain development and learning.

Many of the problems with teacher appraisal stem from its linearity and the way it is divorced from the normal patterns of professional working. Developmental review can take place at any time and as often as is necessary; a newly appointed curriculum leader will have very different needs to a headteacher approaching retirement. The nature of the learning process as well as the content will be a significant determinant of the rhythm of the review process. To work it has to be personal and individual. Learning cannot be constrained by artificial requirements – while the timetable may help to deliver the curriculum it does not necessarily facilitate learning.

Team learning

The foundation of organisational learning is individual learning but it is mediated through team learning. Senge (1990) defines team learning as:

> . . . the process of aligning and developing the capacity of a team to create the results its members truly desire. It builds on the discipline of developing shared vision. It also builds on personal mastery, for talented teams are made up of talented individuals. (p. 236)

In Senge's model team learning grows out of and reinforces individual learning – the two are mutually supportive. But it is through the team that greater potential can be unlocked.

Few schools have genuine team cultures; usually the term is just a label for a group. For professional learning to achieve its full potential it has to be enhanced through the collaborative working of a genuine team. This is not the context to discuss the full range of organisational issues surrounding the concept of effective teams. Suffice it to say that a team cannot exist or flourish in a control culture and that bureaucracy and hierarchy are anathema to the notion of the autonomous team which has as a prime responsibility improvement through learning.

Team learning takes place when most of the following criteria are met to a significant extent:

1 There is a clear and accepted purpose for the team and a high level of consensus about the values that inform team processes.

2 The team is 'balanced' in the sense that it has been created from people with complementary characteristics who are able to work together effectively.

3 There is an emphasis on the development of process skills as well as task-related skills – i.e. the team develops the capacity to work together as well as to complete the task.

4 When the team is functioning it uses a simple model to guide its behaviour – in essence: Plan → Act → Review. There is shared planning as to who will do what when in advance of actually engaging in the task. Once the strategy has been agreed it is implemented by all members of the team in an appropriate and consistent way. When the task is completed the whole team reviews 'What was achieved?' and 'How was it achieved?'

5 Leadership in the effective team is distributed according to the needs of the situation, so allowing for the development of leadership qualities in a secure environment.

6 The team constantly challenges itself through the setting of new tasks, extending its membership and reinventing the way it works.

7 Individual learning and knowledge is assimilated into the team. There are regular audits of the skills, knowledge and qualities that are available against anticipated demands.

8 The team regularly recognises and celebrates its success and time is spent in reinforcing capability and achievement.

Although effective team learning may need an external impetus from time to time and all teams benefit from working with other teams, the majority of team learning is focused on learning by doing, using the mutually supportive social relationships to encourage creativity, learn from failure and develop new qualities and skills.

In the context of the school the team can facilitate learning in a wide variety of ways, e.g.

● the school leadership team learning to use strategic planning techniques;

● a subject team exploring new assessment strategies and monitoring their implementation;

● a project team carrying out research into parental attitudes and implementing a revised reporting strategy;

- an *ad hoc* team being trained in the use of an integrated learning system and then passing on their understanding to their subject or pastoral teams.

In all cases the whole is greater than the sum of the parts – task completion and social relationships are enhanced and the potential for learning significantly increased.

The school-based programme

Whole-school programmes exist to support professional learning in those situations where there is (a) a need for organisational consistency or (b) it is more cost effective to provide service training. In both cases it could be argued that the use of a training day is a last-resort strategy unless it is firmly contextualised by team and individual learning strategies. There would appear to be a prima facie case to argue that the impact of the traditionally constituted training day is profoundly constrained. If such a day is to move beyond being 'interesting', 'a pleasant change' or 'a good lunch and a chance to talk' then it has to be designed with implementation in mind, i.e. the day is only one component of an extended process which draws on what we know about individual and team-based professional learning.

In order to avoid the 'interesting day but so what?' syndrome, whole-school development activities need to meet the following criteria:

1   They are demonstrably consistent with the school's mission statement and strategic and development plan priorities.
2   There is no alternative or better way to foster professional learning.
3   The session is designed to employ a range of learning strategies.
4   Consultants are employed to work to the school's agenda rather than their own.
5   There are clear strategies for implementation at team and individual level.
6   There is a clear focus on the experience of pupils – in particular their achievement.

In essence any whole-school event should draw on the approaches identified in Chapter 4 and should be capable of rapid implementation. Individual days or events need to be part of an overall strategy which is supportive of a school improvement strategy and is clearly developmental in the sense of having a logical progression which adds value at each stage. However well designed, the whole-school approach will always be constrained by the extent to which it fosters individual learning and so change leading to action.

Darling-Hammond (1997, p. 326) synthesises the key characteristics of developmental strategies that lead to improvement. They tend to be:

- experiential, engaging teachers in concrete tasks of teaching, assessment and observation that illuminate the processes of learning and development;

- grounded in participants' questions, inquiry and experimentation as well as profession-wide research;
- collaborative, involving a sharing of knowledge among educators;
- connected to and derived from teachers' work with their students;
- sustained and intensive, supported by modelling, coaching and problem solving around specific problems of practice;
- connected to other aspects of school change.

7
■ ■ ■

Monitoring and Evaluating Professional Learning

Historically, monitoring and evaluation have been the weakest link in the chain of school improvement and school effectiveness. The reasons for this are complex and varied but the problem is best exemplified by the imposition of external inspections in what was perceived to be a vacuum. This chapter considers the related processes of monitoring and review and argues that they have to be placed in the context of the central processes of learning and improvement. In this sense evaluation is of marginal significance in that it is *post facto* and a powerful exemplification of a linear model of management which produces a judgement at the conclusion of a process or project.

Evaluation can create a false optimism about the nature of improvement. For example, there is no doubt that the evaluation of a new reading scheme or a particular cohort's GCSE results will lead to improvement. However, this is at the expense of those whose experience is being evaluated – there is little comfort in being told that although an experience was bad it will be better for those who follow. This level of altruism is neither valid nor appropriate! This chapter therefore considers evaluation as a tool but argues that sustained self-review and a strategy based on prevention are more appropriate.

Monitoring and evaluation

Monitoring has been defined by the Oxford Consortium for Educational Achievement (OCEA, 1996) as:

> ... the collection of information in order to answer the question 'Are we doing what we set out to do?' Information can be collected in a variety of ways ... Monitoring can take place over a variety of timescales depending on its purpose, focus and method. (p. 4)

This is contrasted with evaluation which:

> ... *takes place in order to answer the question 'Is what we are doing worthwhile?' It is the process by which judgements are reached about the outcomes of planned action; how valuable or worthwhile an activity is in relation to the quality of education provided for the learners. It also provides an answer to the question 'How has this action resulted in improvement?' (p. 4)*

Evaluation is thus a historic process which allows judgements to be made on the basis of evidence collected through monitoring. As such it can play a significant role in the analysis of strategic options and in providing evidence for accountability purposes. However, the evaluation process, however intrinsically well managed, is compromised by a number of factors:

- It is summative rather than formative for those actually involved in a specific process, especially if they are children whose timeframe for education is very different to that of professional educators.
- The collection of evidence is potentially problematic and contentious.
- The evidence for an evaluation report can have a significant impact on the nature of the evaluation and the way in which outcomes are reported.
- The status of the evaluation report and the extent to which it is integrated into school management processes will fundamentally determine its significance.
- Most important of all is the authority of an evaluation report's outcomes. The conclusions and recommendations in such reports are often marginalised, if not actually ignored at national as well as institutional level.

Having raised these concerns it is important to stress that there are circumstances where a formal evaluation is both appropriate and desirable, e.g.

- at the conclusion of a specific, time-constrained project, e.g. a school-based award-bearing programme run in conjunction with a local university;
- to establish detailed information about the current state of a particular aspect of a school's management, e.g. levels of satisfaction with existing arrangements for INSET;
- in order to review the status of a particular aspect of provision, e.g. arrangements for consultation with parents.

What evaluation is not appropriate for, in the sense of the definitions cited above, is anything to do with a learning process. This is for two reasons: first, the summative and historic nature of evaluation which makes it inappropriate to 'wait' for findings; second, the fact that evaluation as a process is not consistent with the learning process and therefore does not model or replicate, and so reinforce, the key function of schools.

If it is decided that evaluation is the appropriate methodology to be adopted then a number of key questions need to be answered

1 What is the purpose of the evaluation?

Two broad responses are needed to this question. The first is to determine the actual focus of the evaluation. It is not enough to evaluate the school-based award-bearing course. It has to be evaluated in order to establish the extent to which it met a range of predetermined and specified criteria. One of the biggest problems in the evaluation of professional development activities is that the focus is on satisfaction rather than the attainment of objectives.

Second, the purpose of the evaluation has to be determined in terms of such factors as accountability, contribution to a research project, proving the validity of a particular strategy, etc.

2 What is the audience for the evaluation?

The audience is a fundamental determinant of many of the factors involved in designing an evaluation exercise. For example, there will be significant differences in reports to the governing body, the Teacher Training Agency, the whole staff of the school and to parents and the local community. The key variables to be considered will include:

- the amount of detail reported;
- the language adopted;
- the size and format of the report;
- the formulation of conclusions and recommendations.

3 Who should evaluate?

This is in many ways the central issue. On the one hand there is often the demand associated with evaluation for there to be the legitimacy of objectivity only possible with an external evaluator. On the other hand is the need for those who have been involved in the project being evaluated to be major protagonists in the evaluation as well. Removing them from the process could be seen as artificially truncating their learning as well as indicating a lack of trust in their ability to achieve a level of detachment. There is no doubt that an external perspective can be invaluable, more to ask naive questions than to be objective, but what is essential is that evaluation is a team process – this increases the possibility of learning and will enhance the quality of the actual evaluation.

4 How should the evaluation be conducted?

Much of the evidence necessary to allow a valid evaluation will be derived from the data generated through appropriate monitoring techniques. The choice of technique will be largely determined by the purpose and scope indicated in the brief setting up the evaluation. A second factor will be what Reid and Barrington (1997) refer to as the level of evaluation, i.e.

- **Level 1:** Reactions of trainees to the content and methods of training, to the trainer and to any other factors perceived as relevant.
- **Level 2:** Learning attained during the training period. Did the trainees learn what was intended?
- **Level 3:** Did the learning transfer to the job?
- **Level 4:** Has the training helped departmental performance?
- **Level 5:** Has the training affected the ultimate well-being of the ... organisation?

The level of evaluation will largely determine the methodology and data-gathering techniques selected. If, as is very often the case, evaluation works at a number of levels at the same time then a range of techniques will be required. Virtually any text on research methods in education will provide a comprehensive survey of appropriate investigative strategies. The following list indicates the range of possibilities:

- **Questionnaires:** open or closed, postal or administered, quantitative or qualitative – or a mixture?
- **Interviews:** structured, semi-structured or open?
- **Observation:** see above (p. 83).
- **Document analysis:** management documents, e.g. reports and minutes, letters, diaries and journals.
- **Focus groups:** structured and managed group discussion in order to generate insights and conclusions.
- **Action research:** the reported outcomes of the participants.
- **Client surveys:** similar to questionnaires but with a very limited range of questions.
- **Collection of data:** for example, a range of performance indicators indicating changes or the additions of value in terms of the relevant variables – literacy and numeracy rates, SATs and GCSE results, attendance figures.

The following list provides a checklist for deciding which method of evaluation to choose.

1 Can this method provide the information we are looking for?
2 Will this method be acceptable to the people who will be involved?
3 Have we the time to plan and apply the method properly, including the necessary analysis of the data collected?
4 Is any equipment or back-up support needed and, if so, is it available? (*op. cit.* p. 170).

5 *How will the evidence be interpreted?*

The evaluation process is beset by problems of value, macro and micro political considerations, the impact on the audience and the perceptions (and prejudices) of the evaluator(s). These are the issues that face any project that has research connotations. As such the principles of validity and reliability apply as much to an evaluation report as to any other piece of research. In the specific context of evaluation there are two crucial factors which will determine the integrity of the analysis and the interpretation of data and so of the judgements and conclusions:

- the clarity with which the intentions, purposes and outcomes of the project being evaluated were originally stated;
- the accuracy with which the remit of the evaluation itself has been defined.

If these two elements are clear and unambiguous then the evaluation is likely to be successful and produce valid conclusions and recommendations which can be acted on.

Interpretation may also have to take into account a range of other factors if it is to produce a valid outcome, e.g. statutory requirements, other available research, previous evaluations and possible precedents for future evaluation exercises.

6 *How will the findings of the evaluation be implemented?*

This depends to a very large extent on how the evaluation is built into the school's planning and review cycle. It also depends, of course, on resource considerations. If the outcomes of an evaluation are to have any effect then they have to be incorporated into the school's strategic and/or development planning cycles as appropriate. The extent to which this is achieved will be largely determined by the following factors:

- the significance attached to the project being evaluated, the credibility of the evaluators and the perceived validity and accessibility of the outcomes;
- the extent to which existing school procedures can accommodate the evaluation process;
- the practicality and specificity of the outcomes.

These three factors are clearly functions of the extent to which a school has a culture which makes evaluation a valued activity. Summative evaluations are unlikely to contribute towards the creation of such culture – indeed, in their most instrumental form they can be regarded as manifestations of the immature organisation (see p. 89 above). It is therefore necessary to explore strategies which move the school towards organisational maturity and are consistent with the twinned notions of the learning organisation and professional learning.

Self-review

Evaluation as discussed in the first section of this chapter was characterised as essentially summative – self-review is characterised, by contrast, as being fundamentally formative. The two approaches may be contrasted as follows:

Summative	Formative
Historic, *post facto*	Current
Grafted on	Systematic
Often external	Internal
Fixed	Evolutionary
Product focused	Process focused
'One-off'	Continuous

As argued above, summative evaluations do have a place but they are essentially constrained. Formative self-review is far more appropriate for professional learning because:

● it is itself a model of the learning process in that it is both iterative and heuristic;

● it becomes part of a process so that changes and development are implicit to the process;

● it allows for continual adjustment and modification in response to experience and reflection;

● it increases the possibility of a project or activity being modified in order to achieve its objectives;

● it reinforces, endorses and authenticates the personal review process;

● most importantly: improvement cannot be inspected or evaluated in.

It is this last point that is central to the rationale for self-review – real change requires high levels of involvement, commitment and acceptance of the need to change. Improvement is in direct correlation with the capacity to engage in appropriate change – as it is with the individual so it is with the organisation, which can only improve as a product of individual improvement and growth in effectiveness. The function of self-review is to support the changes necessary to implement strategies for improvement – in this sense it fulfils exactly the same function for the organisation as reflection does for the individual. Fullan's (1993) 'Eight Basic Lessons of the New Paradigm of Change' demonstrate the symbiotic relationship between change and learning (pp. 21–3):

- Lesson one: You can't mandate what matters.
- Lesson two: Change is a journey not a blueprint.
- Lesson three: Problems are our friends.
- Lesson four: Vision and strategic planning come later.
- Lesson five: Individualism and collectivism must have equal power.
- Lesson six: Neither centralisation nor decentralisation works.
- Lesson seven: Connection with the wider environment is critical.
- Lesson eight: Every person is a change agent.

All of these lessons demonstrate the highly contingent nature of change and the number of variables which impact upon the process. In this respect change and learning are identical but in the context of school improvement perhaps the most important is that 'you can't mandate what matters'. Improvement, like learning, cannot be imposed.

Rosenholtz (1991) points to the importance of linking learning and improvement:

> *In learning-enriched settings, an abundant spirit of continuous improvement seemed to hover schoolwide, because no one ever stopped learning to teach. Indeed, clumped together in a critical mass, like uranium fuel rods in a reactor, teachers generated new technical knowledge, the ensuing chain reaction of which led to greater student mastery of basic skills. Principals' frequent and useful evaluations seemed also a powerful mechanism for delivery on the promise of school improvement as they also served as guides for future work. (p. 208)*

It is this last sentence that integrates improvement, learning and self-review.

In this model, review is implicit in every stage of the improvement strategy rather than at the end. Planning is constantly modified to take account of what has been learnt from the preceding activity through an intrinsic review process. If the same questions that were applied to evaluation in the first section of this chapter are applied to self-review then it is possible to develop a detailed picture of the model.

1 **What is the purpose of the review?** Improvement – of both the product *and* the process. The iterative nature of review allows for continuing modification and adjustment of the project under review and the means by which it is being managed. Most importantly both can be changed as soon as it is discovered to be necessary rather than waiting for problems and issues to emerge when the project or activity is completed. This precisely replicates the individual learning process. Evaluation has such credibility because it parallels almost exactly the nature of the assessment process

applied to young people. The process of improvement cannot be artificially curtailed by the attainment of an arbitrary, externally imposed, goal.

2 **What is the audience for the review?** Primarily those involved in the actual process. The outcomes of the review stages can contribute to detailed and comprehensive reports and, if appropriate, to a summative evaluation. The most important and significant use of any review is the extent to which it enables individuals to understand their own work, to reflect on it and so to manage their learning so as to be able to contribute to sustaining institutional and personal improvement.

3 **Who should carry out the review?** Again, everyone involved in the process. If professional learning is to become endemic to school life then participation in process review has to become fundamental to every teacher, manager and leader. Sharing in product and process review is the perfect counterpoint to personal reflection and the interaction between personal and team reflection is one of the most powerful creative dynamics.

4 **How should the review be conducted?** The strategies, principles and techniques for carrying out a review are the same as those for evaluation and for personal reflection. What is important is that those who are involved carry out the data collection in just the way that they would to support their own reflective practice. The review process is substantially enhanced by the process of sharing and the coalition of perspectives and perceptions that is possible when a sophisticated team engages in the process of dynamic review. Team review has a number of potential advantages:

- it is likely to be more critical, analytical and systematic;
- a sophisticated team will be more creative and generate a wider range of strategies;
- the team will create high-level interpersonal skills which will support and facilitate reflection and enhance self-awareness and self-esteem;
- the team will implement solutions.

5 **How will the review be interpreted?** In accordance with the values and principles established at the outset of a particular project or any process that is undertaken in the school. One of the advantages of a systemic review process is that it keeps the core purpose firmly in mind. Interpretation of progress is thus able to combine checking that intentions are being implemented while at the same time ensuring that appropriate improvements can be made.

6 **How will the findings be implemented?** By informing action. The most important factor is that those people who carry out the review are the same as those who are responsible for the planning and who will also carry the play into action. There is thus shared responsibility for diagnosis and remediation, shared creativity and shared accountability – most importantly there is shared commitment.

Prevention

Prevention is a concept drawn from the total quality movement and is best captured in the somewhat intimidating slogans of that movement 'Right first time' and 'Zero defects'. In essence prevention is a management philosophy which is concerned with stopping things going wrong in the first place rather than seeking to put things right. In this respect it is sharply contrasted with both evaluation and self-review in that it is seeking to design a product or process in such a way as to minimise the possibility of deviation from a specification. The fundamental idea is to increase client satisfaction by delivering what has been promised and enhancing organisational effectiveness by reducing 'waste'. In the context of professional development and learning this means increasing confidence that developmental activities actually lead to the change intended and desired.

When applied in an industrial context the concept of waste is easy to envisage – components that don't work, services that fail to achieve published standards. In the educational context it is much more difficult to apply the principle mainly because the variables that apply are so much more complex and, crucially, often totally outside the control of the school. It is comparatively simple for a large commercial organisation to insist that its suppliers deliver goods which conform to a precise, and easily measurable, set of specifications. Supermarkets can define the ideal carrot and take steps to ensure it is supplied. Schools are not in the same position when it comes to children. However, in a number of cases it is possible to move away from a resigned acceptance to a more proactive stance and professional development is one of these areas.

Prevention revolves around the notion of assurance – increasing confidence that what is intended is actually delivered. Failure to meet a specification leads to variation which will diminish client satisfaction and increase costs. In the context of professional learning and development variation can take a number of forms:

- a course that does not cover the advertised content;
- a school development day that does not include strategies for consistent application across the whole school;
- a development programme that does not recognise and respond to individual differences;
- a skills-based programme which does not include provision for implementation and coaching;
- an award-bearing programme that has no relationship with the school-based experience of participants;
- appropriate content poorly presented/inappropriate content well presented.

In all of these cases there is divergence from what is presumed to be the primary purpose of developmental activities – creating the potential to change and to translate principle into practice. In order to minimise or eliminate variation four principles have to be applied to the management of professional development and learning (West-Burnham, 1997, p. 68):

1 Explicit definition of standards.

2 Consistent application of best practice procedures.

3 Monitoring and measurement.

4 Use of corrective action.

Each of these principles will now be applied to the management of professional development and learning.

1 Explicit definition of standards

This principle is at the heart of prevention and quality assurance and it all hinges on the notion of design – the quality principle of 'fitness for purpose'. In order to achieve 'fitness' the purpose has to be clearly understood and in the total quality environment the purpose can only be that of the client or customer. A similar concept is the notion of 'conformance to requirements' where the requirements are those of the client and conformance is achieved through establishing the requirements and then designing the process to ensure conformance.

Oakland (1993) describes the Quality Function Deployment (QFD) system as a means of designing a service which meets customer needs and involves all those in the 'supplier organisation'. He describes the activities as (p. 48):

1 Market research

2 Basic research

3 Invention

4 Concept design

5 Prototype testing

6 Service testing

7 After-sales service.

In essence the whole process can be reduced to three questions (p. 49):

- *Who* are the customers?
- *What* does the customer need?
- *How* will the needs be satisfied?

In the context of professional development and learning these principles can be translated into the following specific criteria:

1 Content, methods and outcomes have to be specifically designated.

2 Learning strategies have to be articulated and individual rather than generic.

3 The target audience has to be precisely defined.

4 Preparation and implementation strategies have to be made explicit as part of programme design.

5 Strategies for monitoring and review have to be implicit to the design.

6 Criteria for success have to be agreed at the outset.

The principles for the design of professional learning and development activities can be encapsulated into a number of questions which help to establish the design parameters of the activity:

1 What changes will result from engaging in the activity?

2 What are the performance indicators that will be used to judge the success of the activity?

3 How will individual learning styles be incorporated into the design and delivery of the programme?

4 What is the relationship between knowledge and skills and how does this inform the design and delivery of the programme?

5 How will participant feedback be built into the improvement of the programme?

6 What strategies will be used to establish the prior learning of participants?

7 How will the aims and outcomes be defined so as to attract an appropriate cohort?

8 What will be the relationship between didactic and experiential approaches, tutor-led and participant-led activity?

It is only through obtaining answers to questions like these that it becomes possible to obtain an explicit definition of standards and so reduce the possibility of failure (and waste) and increase the confidence that a professional development activity is 'fit for purpose'.

2 Consistent application of best practice procedures

Following the process of client-focused design and the associated monitoring it becomes possible to define best practice. This approach often appears under the guise of benchmarking and in essence is a strategy to ensure that, when variables are found to be consistent, proven techniques are employed in order to avoid the 'waste' of perpetual reinvention.

For professional development purposes best practice will emerge through the consolidation of programmes, events and strategies that have actually been proven to work and their application to a new context. This implies a very high degree of sophisticated communication in a school in order to capture best practice in a variety of contexts. The experience of hearing a visionary and inspirational speaker at a conference may not translate into a practically focused school-based training day. Equally, a higher education programme might be a transformational experience for one teacher and a succession of banal platitudes for another.

However, it is possible to conceptualise a situation where a school builds up accumulated wisdom as to what works and what does not. Indeed this already happens in most schools but often in a random and haphazard way. What is needed is the creation of a portfolio of best practice which might include:

- presenters and facilitators
- strategies and techniques
- venues and organisational arrangements
- support and follow-up.

Just as each major motor-car manufacturer buys its rival's latest model and takes it apart to judge its own models against so schools need to disassemble their in-service education providers and measure them against an explicit standard.

Prevention is achieved by specifying a standard and then ensuring consistent application of that standard so as to minimise variation. Such a specification depends on adequate definition of requirements. The major source for such definitions in this context would be the mission statement, job descriptions and a policy for professional learning and development. Necessary definitions would include:

1 the principles and components of learning-in-action;
2 the role of the teacher, manager and leader as learner;
3 the criteria used to inform the selection of development activities so that they model best classroom practice;
4 the nature and purpose of coaching and its place in improving practice;
5 the nature and purpose of reflexive learning.

Such an approach inevitably brings with it the danger of bureaucracy and a 'Standard Operating Procedures Manual' so comprehensive and detailed that nobody can carry it – let alone refer to it. The level of definition will be a direct reflection of organisational maturity – the thicker the manual the greater the immaturity. But it may be necessary to pass through a transitional phase – from ostensive definition to a value-driven consensus.

3 Monitoring and measurement

Much of what was written in the preceding sections of this chapter applies to this topic, in particular the role of monitoring as a continuous data-collection activity to inform managers of the extent to which an activity is 'on-track'. While quantitative data is seductive, and often appropriate, in this context qualitative data, especially the perceptions of participants, is valid and vital.

Certain activities will lend themselves to easy measurement and rapid confirmation. For example, training in such strategies as the use of an Integrated Learning System or Reading Recovery can be monitored because of the quantifiable outcomes that both approaches lend themselves to. However, it is much more complicated to judge the impact of a HEADLAMP programme or NPQH training. In such cases, where the criteria and provision are generic, then the perceptions of the participant will be of primary significance.

Quantitative satisfaction ratings do provide some feedback – but often only on the quality of the catering. Unless the principles set out in the first two parts of this section are applied then measurement in order to check consistency is impossible.

4 Use of corrective action

In an industrial environment this refers to an intervention to correct a process that systematic measurement has shown to be working inappropriately. The important point is that intervention takes place during the process in order to ensure that the final outcome is 'fit for purpose'.

This represents a profound move away from the tolerance of inappropriate provision in the hope that 'things might improve' or 'we can adapt ...'. This type of intervention is possible because of the previous three criteria in this section. The combination of definition, best practice working and monitoring allows for specific and timely interventions in order to minimise the possibility of failure.

Effective corrective action depends on an understanding of the purpose of the activity and knowledge of appropriate strategies based on analysis of the dysfunctional element. Examples of the sort of situations where this approach might be valid could include:

- breakdown in the relationship between coach and teacher;
- limited impact of an award-bearing programme;
- a school-based development day failing to secure the involvement of staff;
- an external consultant failing to function effectively.

Intervention offers important parallels with classroom practice – the effective teacher does not wait until the end of a module, term or year to discover failure. The process of monitoring provides the evidence to justify and specify interventions. The predisposition to do this is fundamental to a philosophy of prevention rather than the lamenting of failure.

Conclusion

There is no doubt that formal evaluation is necessary in a strategic context and for accountability purposes. However, for the purposes of improvement it is necessary to move towards a culture of self-review. At a more fundamental level, and given the scarcity of resources and the significance of the outcomes, professional development and learning has to move into a culture based on prevention. There is not the money, time or energy to contemplate wastage, especially when the implications for pupil achievement and school improvement are so high.

At the very least the costs of evaluation need to become a significant factor in designing the strategy to ensure that school and individual intentions are being translated into actual practice which impacts on performance.

8
■ ■ ■

Implementing Successful CPD – Case Studies

Introduction

This chapter draws together a range of approaches to CPD in a number of different contexts. We offer these as 'starters for 10' rather than blueprints to be followed to the letter. We have tried to cover different stages in a teacher's career, from induction to headship, as well as including an international dimension. We are greatly indebted to our co-authors for permission to précis their original work and would recommend the reader to refer to the original sources for further details of the projects and innovations described. There is no significance in the order of these case studies – all are equally valuable and can be read in any order.

The first example is co-authored by the director of the project and describes an innovative approach to school improvement in very small rural schools, a field where there is both extreme pressure in integrating all the changes which came in the period following the Education Reform Act and a distinct lack of current research. The case study describes the outcomes of a county project run under the Grants for Education Support and Training (GEST) School Improvement priority, in which 42 primary schools of 60 or fewer pupils received £1000 to buy time, resources and training to develop priorities identified through their Development Plans. The main outcomes relate to the value of using earmarked moneys to buy specific resources for the group of pupils targeted and time for teaching heads and staff to plan, implement and evaluate. The project was a collaborative one and all participants, at school and LEA level learned much about the process of systematic but flexible development.

This is followed by a study of two contrasting approaches to staff development in secondary schools, one written in collaboration with the headteacher and the other from the point of view of the leader of the centre described. These two mini case studies look at different approaches to professional development in two secondary schools. The first involves one GM secondary school and all the senior and middle management over a two-year period. A taught course was provided by the local LEA on each unit of the RSA middle management (NVQ Level 4) syllabus. The senior management worked towards Level 5 as well as co-ordinating the programme. At the later stages outside help was commissioned by the LEA to assist participants to collect, collate and prepare their portfolios for assessment. Three participants dropped out (one senior manager and two middle managers) but all others gained their Management NVQs. However, the evaluation conducted by an external HEI identified several key issues in adopting this style of CPD as well as some very positive factors in a coherent approach to CPD at the school level.

The second mini-study reports on the establishment and operation of an in-house professional development centre (the Uden Centre) based in a GM secondary school – the St Thomas the Apostle College in south-east London. In this case the emphasis is on meeting the immediate development needs of the teachers and children in the school. The Centre was originally set up with funds from the TVEI project and early provision was in direct response to the pressures perceived at the time. From this rather *ad hoc* beginning the centre has adopted a more coherent approach, with a core of IT INSET provision and a range of staff development opportunities linked to pupil improvement, organisational development and accreditation through HE for levels from initial teacher training to masters awards.

The next study is based in the Netherlands and is written by one of the key tutors involved in the programme. It involves a network of schools in upper secondary education (15–18 year olds) and a local Institute of In-Service Education working on a course designed to explore the implications of government plans to introduce a modular approach to the curriculum and assessment in upper schools. The participants in the network meetings are upper secondary education co-ordinators, management staff and careers counsellors and members of task forces. Each network organises a minimum of six meetings a year. In 1993/4 work groups were formed to pursue collectively agreed themes: 'towards active learning', 'teaching time' (lesson duration) and 'the third grade as the transition from lower to upper general education'. Institute inputs included consultancy, training courses, counselling, educational task forces, small research projects with teachers and discussion meetings with whole staff. Lessons are drawn out about the nature of partnership, influencing government policies, developing together a new education and developing relationships in the network. And the advantages for the participating schools.

The fourth study is an account of an LM school's experience of working collaboratively with the LEA to set up arrangements for appraisal. It is written from the point of view of the appraisal co-ordinator in the school. The school carried out an analysis of the cultures present among the staff and discusses these different cultures, the interactions between the sections of the school and the dominant culture of each section. It highlights the role of the school's staff development committee in taking the lead in planning the implementation of appraisal on behalf of their colleagues. The collaboration between the members of the committee and between them and the appraisal co-ordinator is identified as a key feature of the successful introduction of appraisal. This is an interesting study given that appraisal is likely to become an important arm of the Labour government's strategy for school improvement in the years leading up the millennium.

The final case study tackles the key issue of the induction and support of beginning teachers and is written by one of the main tutors involved in the programme. It is based in the northern region of Israel and concerns a project run by Haifa Technion, the Israel Institute of Technology, involving eight beginning science teachers in the first year, 16 in the second and 22 in the third, and their respective mentors. The project examines the various models available for supporting teacher induction and develops a new model synthesising aspects from around the world. The project was formally evaluated through interviews, feedback and attitude questionnaires. The project identifies ways of surmounting the special obstacles encountered by new science teachers in their first year of teaching. Lessons about the process of creating a learning culture through the involvement of teachers, mentors and HE tutors are drawn out as well as practical suggestions for teachers. Only one student of those who went through the programme dropped out of teaching during the period of the study.

There are many lessons to be drawn from these case studies. They are representative only in the sense that there is a range of approaches and contexts. In our experience it is more important that those responsible for staff development and school improvement do some preliminary research to determine what there is available already in the field and then get on and *do* something! All the schools and other partners reported here got a lot out of the action project in which they were involved but the examples are inevitably context-bound. We suggest you take your own lessons from the outcomes of these projects and get on and do something of your own – but please remember to keep open your collective enquiring minds. It is the things *you learn* which are the most powerful outcomes.

Case Study 1
The Lincolnshire Small Schools Project
Muriel George

Introduction

The participants in this case study were the Education Leadership Centre of a new university campus in a rural county city in eastern England, the Education and Cultural Services Directorate of the county council and the 42 schools directly involved in the project itself. The initiative was delivered during the 1996–97 financial year to match the GEST cycle, though in the summer term of 1997 a summative questionnaire was issued to the schools' headteachers, chairs of governors and advisory staff and a preliminary report of the findings of the project plus ten case studies of good practice was prepared.

Methodology

The approach to the project evaluation is qualitative and interpretative in nature and can be described as action enquiry. This consists of a series of cycles of data generation prompted by four key questions (McNiff, 1988; O'Sullivan, 1995):

1 What is the field of enquiry?

2 What is our current practice?

3 How can we improve our practice?

4 What have we learned about improving our practice?

In this study one of the co-authors (from the university partner) acted as the researcher/evaluator constructing the evaluation methodology in consultation with the client and agreeing how each stage of the evaluation would proceed – the timescale involved, the data collection techniques, analysis methods and arrangements for feedback to the participants at the completion of each cycle of enquiry. The emphasis is on reflection on professional action for the purposes of improvement in professional practice and the validation of this through the presentation of preliminary findings and discussion with the practitioners. Subsequent cycles of activity and enquiry are thus informed by previous stages and a consensus developed which grounds the enquiry firmly in the ongoing reality of practice (Berger and Luckman, 1996; Strauss and Corbin, 1990).

This approach is not strictly action research as, although the school participants were engaged in gathering data and responding to the analysis and presentation of preliminary findings, they were not asked to incorporate these into their practice and then report on the outcomes. The scope of the evaluation in terms of timescale and resources precluded more than one cycle of action. Also the researcher was acting as a contracted evaluator and did not take part in the field of practice directly other than as a non-participant observer.

However, there are features of this study which do replicate the action research cycle to a greater extent, for example the relationship between the researcher/evaluator and the project steering group (this consisted of the project director – the other co-author of this case study – a senior county adviser and five headteachers seconded to the project for the year). The initial approach was made by the senior county adviser (as a result of contacts made between the new Lincoln University campus and the County Education and Cultural Services Directorate) and the evaluation proposal and budget were agreed through negotiation. Once the evaluation commenced, the researcher/evaluator attended most of the steering group meetings and advised on the internal evaluations strategy. He also attended a sample of school review meetings, feedback meetings and the evaluation conference.

The project context

The programme concerns a group of small schools in the rural English county of Lincolnshire. There are national as well as local issues involved as the funding for the development was provided as part of the 1996/7 GEST year grant from the Department for Education and Employment (DfEE) while the LEA (in this case Lincolnshire County Council) provided the project team and framework for the programme. The following account outlines the context and history of the project.

In 1994 Lincolnshire restructured its curriculum and monitoring section to help schools cope with the OFSTED inspection cycle and as part of the 'school improvement' debate. The LEA agreed to take an active role in the national school improvement initiative and carried out a programme of visits to schools, covering headteacher appraisal, curriculum monitoring, performance analysis and school development planning. Alongside this a professional development programme with courses, and school-based and cluster-based training was also offered. On the school improvement and target-setting front, the LEA published comparative indicators and an analysis of each school's statutory teacher assessments, task and test results. A number of initiatives were also begun, for example: primary literacy, primary numeracy, management development, drug education in the primary school and the value added dimension.

From this general service provided by the LEA to all its schools, the Small Schools Improvement Project emerged. These schools are a particular feature in the county as Lincolnshire is sparsely populated with a large number of geographically isolated settlements. Because of the small number of pupils in such schools, the GEST funding formula is barely able to cover all aspects of the National Curriculum, appraisal, assessment, IT, LMS and governor training. Many of these grants, when devolved to schools on a per capita basis, give such small amounts in very small schools that, because they are often 'earmarked' for specific purposes, the school is unable to respond to the individual needs of the pupils and staff at any particular time.

Thus, small schools have far fewer options when considering staff development, co-ordination and support. Headteachers of these small schools are also class teachers with a weekly allocation for their headteacher role of often only one half-day and they are therefore even more stretched managerially.

The county council recognised the particular circumstances of small schools and the project enabled the LEA to provide enhanced support beyond that which is already available. The programme was designed to offer a partnership with the 42 primary schools with 60 or fewer pupils on roll to work with them through a structured process to help them move towards school improvement. The central aim for the project was 'To enable schools to raise standards for all pupils'.

The particular problems identified with the small schools and which the project hoped to address were:

- the isolation of the schools and the community;
- the pressures on the staff to deliver the curriculum;
- the lack of time and flexibility to become involved in LEA initiatives;
- the demands placed on teachers to meet specialisms, particularly at Key Stage 2;
- the planning requirements to meet the differentiated needs of ability and age covering 3–4 years in one class;
- limited financial flexibility in staff development and resource planning;
- early years curriculum planning and delivery;
- monitoring and evaluation of the quality of teaching and learning;
- variation in standards and achievement in different subject areas.

In order to move forward on these issues a contract was devised and agreed with each school, setting out both the LEA's obligations and the school's commitment to their own focus within the project.

Stage 1: Audit of performance at school level

One element of the contract with the LEA was that the schools would undertake Performance Indicators in Primary Schools (PIPS) assessments in order to provide more detailed information about the characteristics of their intakes.

All 42 schools have administered the PIPS baseline assessment to the children in their reception classes. The results were standardised against the total number of pupils from Lincolnshire schools to whom the baseline assessment was administered and this allowed the schools to see how their results compared with those of other schools within the LEA. The schools also received their own results plotted against the national results. In addition the schools have administered the Y2 and Y6 PIPS tests in the spring term and these results have also enabled the schools to compare their results against the LEA norm and the national norm.

Because the project in Lincolnshire is dealing with small cohorts of pupils, the PIPS data has been exceedingly useful for schools to enable them to consider individual children's performance and attainment, given their contextual scores, and to compare them with LEA and national norms.

These data have been analysed and used by the schools:

- to identify those children who appeared at both extremes of the ability scales, i.e. those in the highest- and lowest-scoring 2.5 per cent of the national cohort;
- to ensure that a range of activities was being planned for all children and that these activities matched the children's abilities as identified through this test;
- to ensure that their curriculum particularly focused on the areas of weakness where there were significant differences in children's performances in maths and reading and science (Y6 only).

Advisory staff from the LEA have provided training and support for schools in analysing their data and have attempted to :

- work with the schools to interpret their results;
- help them integrate this information into a self-evaluation process which is a prerequisite to their school development planning;
- lead them into using the results to set targets.

Stage 2: Provision and use of benchmark and comparative information

The LEA now has a range of data which will be used in the next academic year to group schools with similar characteristics. These data comprise:

- Key Stage 1 statutory results for all schools at individual and school level for 1994 and almost complete data for 1991–3;
- Key Stage 2 statutory results at school level for 1995 and 1996 and complete results at individual pupil level for 1997;

- PIPS results for baseline assessments for all 42 small schools in the project and also for 130 other LEA schools;

- PIPS results for Y2, Y4 and Y6 pupils for over half the schools in the LEA including the 42 schools in the project;

- results from a National Foundation for Educational Research in England and Wales (NFER) test which is administered annually to all pupils in Y4 as part of the LEA procedures for moderating the SEN register;

- additional data from a range of sources which impact on the performance of individual schools, e.g. provision of Free School Meals, English as an Additional Language pupils, information about pupil mobility, Pre-Inspection Contextual and School Indicators (an OFSTED document produced from national and local statistics prior to a formal inspection), etc.

The data collected so far will allow for the grouping of schools in the future, so that the LEA can provide each school with benchmark statistics which take into account the local context. This will enable schools to make meaningful comparisons of their statutory assessments with those from schools sharing similar characteristics.

Value added

The data that the initiative has generated will be analysed within a value-added framework. The key unit of measurement is the progress each pupil at school has made during the first and subsequent two-year periods. Schools in the project, in the first and second year of PIPS testing, will receive results which show 'relative value added' and in the third year of testing, results will be available showing actual value added.

In addition, in 1997, the LEA has offered a data processing service for schools with Y6 pupils. In return for providing schools with printouts of pupils' results and school summary results, the LEA has begun to build up a database of Key Stage 2 results at individual pupil level for future value-added work.

Stage 3: Using information to set targets for improvement – the Action Enquiry

The project has been managed by a steering group which has endeavoured to:

- minimise the administrative burden to schools;
- assist the schools in interpreting information;
- lead the schools through the target-setting process;
- play a role in the ongoing monitoring of progress.

The schools taking part in the project agreed an area of focus. A contract was devised setting out both the LEA's obligations and each school's chosen area(s) of focus. This was discussed and approved with the governing body of each school. After the focus had been agreed an audit was conducted at each school by the headteacher, a representative of the governors, the school adviser and a member of the steering group for the project. The audit considered the following:

- the whole school development plan;
- the quality of teaching and learning;
- continuity and progression in the curriculum;
- the professional development of the staff;
- the role of the governing body.

As a result key targets for each school were identified and criteria agreed that could describe how success in meeting the targets would have changed the performance of the school. An agreed action plan was also drawn up at these meetings and this identified:

- what action was required by members of staff, LEA support staff, the school advisor, the governors, etc.;
- who had responsibility for the action;
- the timescale;
- what resources were necessary, e.g. human, financial, etc., within the allocated budget of £1000; and finally
- how the initiative was going to be monitored and evaluated in each school.

An emphasis was placed on the clarity of these plans and intentions so that all staff and governors could share in the overall process. Challenging yet achievable targets were set and regular monitoring of progress was built into the action plans. There followed a joint evening meeting with headteachers and governors to agree the targets and proposed action.

Identification of strategies to improve teaching and learning to reach targets

Following the meetings with headteachers and governors where each school's action plan was formally agreed, the project director analysed the 42 schools' action plans in order to collate the support required.

In-service training was arranged for schools with similar targets, and the team has also helped with co-ordinating schools' individual INSET needs and liaising with advisory teachers and other external agencies. Schools were able to draw on the following support in order to achieve their targets:

- the LEA's advisers and advisory teachers to help with staff development and give advice on curriculum, management, finance or resourcing matters;
- LEA advisory teachers to deliver school-based INSET tailored to each school's individual needs, e.g. working with children and teachers to demonstrate technology, running training days, staff meetings and/or parents evenings on specific issues, organising agreement trialling with a cluster of schools to look at consistency in assessment standards;
- attendance on LEA-designated courses or short courses as appropriate;
- use of individuals or agencies to help in achieving targets, e.g. the LEA Reading Recovery Team;
- meetings for heads and governors to share information and discuss the aims of the project;
- visits to other schools to view resources, share approaches, develop networks, etc.

Some examples of the types of additional support which were organised are outlined below:

- a joint in-service training day was provided on 'Developing Children's Writing' for the teachers from six schools which had identified En3 as a focus;
- four of the schools with IT as their area for development have formed a support group which has met regularly for mutual support as well as the INSET which has been provided;
- five of the schools have purchased computers with CD-ROM facilities and a member of the LEA support services has worked in these schools with teachers and children to enable them to become familiar and confident with the technology;
- three of the schools which were concerned with assessment issues, particularly to do with consistency of standards, have worked together with LEA advisory staff on agreement trialling and have produced a joint portfolio of assessed work;
- the LEA Reading Recovery Team offered specific targeted support to schools which had identified standards in reading as a key issue.

Outcomes from the project

Although there are many outcomes from this project which apply particularly to small schools and their specific problems, the evaluation has identified a number of key outcomes which are applicable to any school district considering embarking on a school improvement programme.

Evaluation of improvement

Monitoring and evaluation procedures were agreed at the outset of the project and a formal evaluation by an external consultant (the evaluator/researcher) is currently nearing completion. Initial findings were collated from:

- an analysis of the written reports following the review meetings (such meetings were held with headteachers, sector advisers, steering group members and sometimes governors throughout the project);

- findings from steering group meetings which were held on a regular basis to evaluate progress;

- responses to a questionnaire which was sent to all schools towards the end of the project;

- findings from a one-day conference which was held in March when part of the day consisted of a sharing of perceptions and a more formal evaluation.

From all of these sources there was an emerging view of the success of the project. Generally the schools have found the initiative to have been valuable and they attribute its perceived success to:

- the high profile the project has received within the county which has raised the status of small schools;

- the support they have received from the LEA;

- the funding which has enabled them to buy additional resources including time.

There were a large number of positive factors identified, the most significant of which were the value of additional resources and support from advisory teachers. Many schools identified as important the ability to use the extra resource to buy time for teachers to meet and the synergy of a concerted effort by external advisory staff, teachers, parents, governors and children on a specific target.

Schools also highlighted the value of focusing on a small group of children and welcomed the administrative and professional help from the steering group. Further positive outcomes of the project were the value of professional dialogue with colleagues from outside the school and the opportunity to visit other schools with similar interests as well as the importance of INSET, both within the school and from courses, for teachers.

Other factors mentioned were:

- the emphasis on audit as a starting point;
- the usefulness of the target-setting, monitoring, review framework;
- the generally positive attitudes of all involved;
- the focus on policy review;
- the tight timescale which ensured implementation;
- the use of PIPS;
- the value for the whole school of this approach.

Issues in implementing the process

Schools felt there was much of value in the project. There was much support for the idea of using the process of target setting in other areas of the curriculum and in the SDP and there was a recognition of the value of aligning the SDP with specific targets through the experience of the project. Other positive factors which emerged were:

- the value of the professional dialogue that the project had brought about;
- the high achievement of pupils and staff involved in the project;
- increasing staff confidence;
- the potential value of schools/headteachers with similar interests meeting and working together;
- the ability to build on existing developments;
- the involvement/understanding of children in the project and use of target setting with them;
- the value of a focus on small schools who feel they are often ignored.

Successful schools are using the principles of the project to review their planning, implementation and evaluation strategies and, from a close focus on a fairly narrow target, are beginning to align their development work with other aspects of policy and planning.

Plans for future development

While acknowledging that the initial funding was important in initiating assisted self-review for the schools, there is a recognition that it is the *process* which has been developed with the schools which will be important in taking the work of the project forward.

Many of the strengths of the project which have been highlighted above will be carried on into the second and third year without having resourcing implications. Future and ongoing support for these schools will comprise:

- their continued involvement with the PIPS project;
- ongoing support from the LEA to analyse and interpret the school's own data;
- the provision of data from similar schools for benchmarking purposes;
- commitment from the schools' advisers to the process of school review, setting and action planning;
- networking with other similar schools for INSET, support, etc.;
- involvement of the schools' advisers in monitoring the action plans and reviewing the progress made; thus
- carrying schools forward in the cycle of continuous improvement.

LEA strategies for improvement

Following the success of the Small Schools Project, the LEA is building on these achievements and the lessons learned in order to extend the principles and processes eventually to all schools. The Curriculum and Monitoring Branch has agreed a rationale for school self-improvement in Lincolnshire. This is set out below:

A key function of the County Council is to assist its schools in the process of self-improvement. We aim to achieve this through helping schools to:

- *review performance across a range of key areas;*
- *evaluate performance in order to identify strengths and weaknesses;*
- *identify specific priorities for action;*
- *set clear and appropriate targets and success criteria for improvement;*
- *monitor and evaluate progress.*

The principles for effective partnership of the school and the LEA in working towards school self-improvement in Lincolnshire are:

1. *The shared development plan is at the heart of the process.*
2. *The agenda for improvement should be negotiated and shared.*
3. *The review will draw upon a range of evidence and include objective data.*
4. *The process will be manageable and sustainable.*
5. *We will work within an agreed framework.*
6. *We will promote a culture of self-review and improvement.*

Having established a rationale and principles for working with all schools, over one-third of the LEA schools have been invited to take part in the LEA School Self-Improvement Pilot Project which was initiated in the second half of the summer term 1997.

Case Study 2(a)
School-based Middle Management Development through NVQs
John Ley

Context

The Blessed Edward Oldcorne Roman Catholic Comprehensive High School is a co-educational, voluntary-aided comprehensive day school serving the area of Worcester city and neighbouring towns in the south of Worcestershire. There are around 890 pupils aged 11–16 on roll. The school has a principal, deputy principal, two assistant principals and some 47 other teachers. It has been commended for the quality of the education offered to pupils in the school's OFSTED report. The school uses a number of training providers in its quest for high-quality INSET for all the staff and has developed a training programme arising from needs identified in the school development plan.

One of these needs was to provide an opportunity for management development, particularly for those with middle management responsibilities. After approaching Hereford and Worcester LEA's Inspection, Advice and Training Service, a development programme was agreed which, in the event, was to combine middle management with the senior managers in an integrated series of lectures and support leading to accreditation at Levels 4 and 5 of the NVQ through the RSA structure for management competencies.

Aims

The programme aimed to help the 14 middle and senior management participants develop or confirm their competence in aspects of their managerial role and to be able to demonstrate and validate this competence to an internal and external assessor. Specifically the programme should:

1 develop and accredit the competence of the middle and senior management staff involved;

2 ensure that participants acquired the necessary underpinning knowledge and understanding;

3 support staff in applying their knowledge, understanding and skills in discharging their responsibilities.

In doing this, the potential benefits for individuals and the school were identified as:

Individual benefits	*School benefits*
• Recognition of their own management achievements	• Promotion of a development culture

- Enhanced confidence in management learning
- Taking a more active role in their own professional development
- Performing more effectively as managers of children's learning

- Enhanced quality management
- Provision of a coherent, common language for management development
- A cost-effective solution to in-house professional development
- Making public the managerial capacity and potential for staff

The emphasis was to be on the collection, collation and presentation of evidence of the application of relevant management knowledge, skills and understanding to a range of practical, school-based contexts backed up by a reflective commentary. The presentation of their portfolio of evidence would be linked to the national standards of competence at the middle management and senior management levels.

In order to enable a sense of cohesion to develop and to map out the management areas under which the portfolio of evidence was to be submitted, a programme of seminars was drawn up in consultation with the school.

Development programme content

In the RSA programme for NVQ Levels 4 and 5, which is endorsed by the Management Charter Initiative, the key purpose for managers is 'to achieve the organisation's objectives and continuously improve its performance'. Derived from this key purpose are a series of management competencies which are grouped into four functional areas:

1 **Managing operations:**   planning, quality and change.

2 **Managing resources:**   equipment, accommodation and finance.

3 **Managing people:**   personnel, human resource management, conflict.

4 **Managing information:**   information systems, communication and decision making.

These functional areas are, in turn, broken down into competence units which describe what is expected of a competent manager for particular aspects of the job. These units of competence consist of a number of elements of competence each with performance criteria and what are termed 'range statements' which indicate the variety of contexts and approaches in which the element of competence could be demonstrated.

The programme negotiated with the school, and delivered by an experience county inspector, covered the following areas:

- Managing quality
- Managing change
- Managing finance
- Managing recruitment
- Team building
- Managing performance
- Managing relationships
- Managing information
- Managing decision making.

These were delivered in a series of workshops which either took place on INSET days or replaced management meetings in the normal calendar cycle. Suitable topics for these workshops, school-based study and assignments were discussed by the tutor with the group and opportunity was taken to contextualise and locate the competencies in real-work situations.

In achieving the collection of evidence to demonstrate the required competencies for each unit the candidates adopted a model of personal effectiveness which embraces how effective managers do their jobs. These personal competencies include the optimising of results through: planning, managing others, managing oneself and the development of one's intellectual capacity.

The programme was therefore based on needs identified by the school and remained flexible to allow individual choice within the context of the school's objectives and the national standards. The aim was to support individuals in the development of skills, knowledge and understanding and to design and develop an appropriate process of collaborative training, research and evaluation.

Assessment and accreditation

The NVQ assessment process involves making judgements about candidates' competence by reviewing evidence which demonstrates their performance against the national standards. The original plan was for each candidate to be assigned one of three assessor/advisers from the county inspectorate. Opportunities were provided to meet with candidates to discuss and review the development of the portfolio of evidence but these proved to be of variable success due to the lack of assessors' experience in the tasks of portfolio review and advice and their very tight work schedules.

There is the opportunity in the portfolio to present evidence of achievement of the standards in a variety of ways such as:

- assessor reports of observations of work practice;
- candidate reports verified by an assessor or other authority such as a line manager;
- reports by previous employers/colleagues;
- products/outcomes of the everyday work activities of candidates;
- video and/or audio recordings;
- agenda and minutes of meetings;
- endorsed photographs;
- notes of discussions with assessors;
- project reports;
- case studies;
- assignment outcomes or other written questions or knowledge tests.

In the building of this portfolio of evidence, candidates are encouraged to focus on specific activities at work, identify the competencies involved and cross-reference these against the standards to ensure adequate coverage. They are supported by:

- an internal verifier who checks that the candidates and assessors understand clearly what is required to meet the standards as well as ensuring the judgements are valid and consistent;
- an external verifier appointed by the accrediting body (in this case the RSA) to visit the centre organising the award to moderate the judgements against other centres to maintain the national standards.

Although there is no specific time limit in the NVQ process of accreditation, the school set up its programme of tuition and collation of portfolios to take place over an 18-month time period.

Preliminary outcomes

The management development programme was extended into the summer term of 1997 in order to enable further assistance with the presentation of portfolios and it has now come to a successful conclusion in that all who presented portfolios have now gained accreditation, i.e. two at Level 5 (senior management) and nine at Level 4 (middle management). Three of the original participants dropped out for differing professional and personal reasons at the time when there was a crisis of confidence in the project. This concerned the lack of experience of some of the original assessor/advisers in the specifics of the presentation of NVQ portfolios and was overcome by the bringing in of an external consultant who had considerable expertise in both this aspect and in motivating candidates towards successful completion of their portfolios.

The external evaluation, completed through the University of Lincolnshire and Humberside, has identified some clear preliminary findings:

- The involvement of both senior and middle management in working together on a programme of management development is a powerful way of overcoming the 'us and them' syndrome and in achieving a critical mass to sustain development.

- Focusing on real tasks in school as a vehicle for developing skills and understanding is an excellent practical approach to identifying and demonstrating competence.

- Management 'courses', even when delivered in the school, do not necessarily ensure the transfer of new knowledge or skills. They need to be actively tailored to the participants' needs as they develop.

- Although the NVQ approach does wonders for 'putting your life in order' through the preparation of a detailed portfolio, it does not necessarily help you to learn ways of approaching 'next generation' change.

- On the other hand, gaining a 'critical mass' of motivation and collective understanding *does* develop skills of leadership and team working and this is probably the single most valuable outcome to help a school staff to respond to whatever the future brings.

- Partnership is a very powerful engine of change – but the school needs to be the driving partner with a clear focus on student outcomes and the learning experience.

Case Study 2(b)
A School-based Professional Development Centre
Veronica Chalmers

Context

Situated in St Thomas the Apostle College, Nunhead, London, the Uden Centre has grown out of the professional needs of the staff and the very real needs of the pupils. The Uden Centre is the focus for the school's professional development. The centre is named after Bill Uden, founding headteacher of the St Thomas the Apostle College. He was headteacher at the newly built school from 1965 until 1983 and his spirit of caring and excellence live on, not only in the school logo but also in the newly established centre for educational development.

The nature of the Uden Centre

The centre is unique and different because developments arise from the teachers' 'grass-roots' experience. Practitioners run the centre but it began in small ways at first. In 1990 the school had the opportunity, provided by TVEI funds, to tailor-make the INSET needs of the staff. Their professional development was based on a cycle of audit, development plan, implementation and evaluation. IT literacy was a high priority for the staff. They wanted to involve the pupils and be involved themselves in teaching and learning with the aid of the computer. So began the yearly sessions of IT INSET for all the staff focusing on the current innovations in IT such as CD-ROM, the Internet and the usual generic software for wordprocessing, spreadsheets and databases. Each year more and more staff improved their IT skills using our own in-house training.

From the time of the school's successful OFSTED inspection in 1993 the staff were looking at ways to improve. Although this inner-city boys' school annually improved in the GCSE and SATs results, it became obvious that we needed to look at the 'why and how' of our examination improvement. The staff became experts at raising the educational standards achieved by the pupils. An audit showed that the improvements were rooted in: useful recording and assessing, recognition of achievement, targeting and tracking, mentoring, coaching, records of achievement, action plans and what has become termed for us 'the onion skin' model.

In 1996 we wanted to use the Uden Centre for initial teacher training. It was recognised that first of all we needed to learn about our own in-house style of teaching. Following the implementation of our own monitoring process involving lesson observations, it became obvious that the school had adopted a particular style of teaching to meet the needs of our pupils. It must be mentioned that the staff include a variety of teaching styles in their lessons but there is an emphasis towards assembling ideas by fine layering, building up a framework very carefully skin by skin until a fully fledged concept is formed. Many of our children are emotionally and mentally damaged for all sorts of reasons. The staff have ensured that they know and understand each child very well. This enables them to teach to a standard that gently brings the pupil to understand quite difficult concepts. It is the 'onion skin' method that eases the path to learning.

The centre offers courses that the teachers have developed. Teaching rigour, however, is essential, as is the belief that the pupils, who are unique and different, deserve a truly nurturing environment. It says much for the college when pupils openly speak to HMI visitors about the encouragement and individuality that each person is afforded. The result of such care shows in a variety of ways: the politeness, smart appearance and pride at belonging to the school as well as the all important examination results. These are truly the means by which many of our boys have hope for a better future.

Developing the courses

Following on from the strategic development planning that has been ongoing and continuous over the last few years, the fruits of our experiences have enabled us to develop and offer courses in each of the following:

- **Raising the Achievement of Boys:** Basic Skills
- **The Year Head:** Role and Responsibility
- **Timetabling Made Easy**
- **GNVQ:** Planning the Course
- **Raising the Achievement of Boys:** Action Planning
- **IT for the School Secretary**
- **Head of Geography:** Organising a Field Trip
- **Residential Fieldwork** – Cornwall
- **GCSE Geography**
- **Admissions and Exclusions**
- **Vision to Reality:** Development Plans.

We looked at our strengths. This has become a straightforward task based on the school's development planning. Each year time is allocated to a discussion of current education issues and future planning targets. For example, numeracy and literacy have engaged our attention for the past three years. Aware as we were of the boys' need to improve in these two areas, we submitted a successful bid to the Basic Skills Agency. From this developed key word books, times table targets and more recently basic grammar books. These issues now occupy a place in the school's development plan. Last year the school put into place ten whole school targets and one of these included the staff's use of the Uden Centre. This may be in the form of a course run by an outside agency in the Uden Centre or indeed teachers running a course for themselves. Our own Curriculum Team meets regularly to drive the process forward.

Central to the school's success is the pastoral system. With our experience as an inner-city school 'The Year Head: Role and Responsibility' sets out to tell how to anticipate possible problems and ways to solve them when they do occur. Increasingly the role of the year head has become a support for the academic work of the pupils. The course looks at the barriers to learning and ways to overcome them. Our own Pupil Support Unit, funded for the next three years, looks at the way that pupils with behavioural difficulties can be supported. Central to the task is the identification of positive strategies such as setting small targets. As a start a pupil may be asked to bring basic equipment to school each day. Such are the fundamental needs of a few of our pupils. It is through the early identification and remedy of the simpler problems that more difficult ones are anticipated and deflected. The demands of the GCSE places enormous pressure on the pupils and it is through early support that pupils see that they can cope with the organisation of a revision programme and independent study. The course identifies several case studies. These highlight the fact that the pupils' success is largely a question of confidence and belief in themselves as capable people.

Our 'Timetabling Made Easy' course, with materials provided, is about to become accredited by Greenwich University for credit accumulation and transfer scheme (CATS) points. Other centre courses will follow for accreditation. The timetabling course has been most popular since its first run in November and is unique in that it takes the teacher from initial concepts to timetabling with the latest software packages. Materials cover staggered lunches, ten-day timetables, treble and quadruple lessons as well as split-site schools. So little published material exists for the novice or experienced timetabler who wants to go computerised that this course has already attracted interest and consultancy requests.

In the last year of TVEI our funds were used to train a number of staff as assessors and verifiers. Seven staff overall qualified and we are registered as a BTEC centre. Now in its second year our Intermediate GNVQ course in Leisure and Tourism attracts pupils to return to us for one more year. The returners say they feel safe with us. Many are sufficiently confident to go on to a sixth-form college but there are a number who need the further support. The lessons we are drawing about the pupil's needs are clear: confidence, security and a clear programme for achievement. A senior teacher plans our GNVQ course. He has already been booked for consultancy this year on starting up a GNVQ. His first statement to interested schools is that the success of a GNVQ course rests on staff commitment and ownership.

Courses that we run are well established in the school structure, one of which is 'Raising Achievement: Action Plans'. From the time of TVEI, we have employed a consultant to interview all Year 10 and Year 11 pupils and provide them with an action plan. A former senior teacher and adviser with a wealth of knowledge and an approachable manner conducts the interviews. He makes the interview an invaluable part of the pupil's planned progress. Such has been the success of action planning that departments now provide pupils with subject action plans.

The school secretary is such an important person in the running of a school and we cater for their interests in 'IT for the School Secretary'. In particular, this is the case in the primary school where useful IT skills speed up the process of administration. The course that we run for the school secretary keeps them up to date with the latest wordprocessing skills and databases which are so useful for keeping track of results and graphs to explain the progress being made.

Organising a field trip can be an onerous task especially for the new head of department. We set out to give practical advice in 'Organising a Field Trip' and time to see what we do on a field trip in 'Residential Fieldwork'. Primary as well as secondary teachers have expressed that these may be useful courses for them.

We concentrate on turning the vision into a reality while avoiding any meaningless rhetoric or jargon that attempts to disguise the facts. We focus on what the school wants to do, who is involved in the task and how it is implemented and monitored. 'Vision into Reality' is a practical course on encapsulating the intention of the Vision in the strategic plans of the school.

Accrediting professional development: student teachers and continuing professional development

We have become involved in the initial training of teachers in partnership with Greenwich University. Again using staff expertise, we have two senior mentors. Their role is to involve staff in teacher training. Participants are asked to complete a formal written outline of their areas of interest in the process of teacher training. Following on from this we have written a programme based on the needs of inner-city children and the particular ways that they learn. When the student teachers observe lessons they will have a written focus of what to look for: ethos and its effect on learning, the environment and its effect on the pupils, learning techniques and their impact on the students' confidence. Staff have been honing their skills in these areas for a number of years but it has only been recently that we have begun to define our role as trainers.

Eighteen teachers at varying stages in their careers support our MA in Education, accredited by Greenwich University. The course includes a practical unit on Research Methodology and credits 15 CATS points towards the MA. In addition six teachers already have a further degree and three are now working towards an MPhil. We intend to hold in-house research within the centre. In particular we are moving towards the development of research in a number of topical areas such as: classroom observation, quality management, added value in a boys' school and raising achievement.

Conclusion

It must be remembered that the courses came out of our INSET audit and staff development – they are based on the needs of teachers in the field. Of course, we cannot meet all training needs but we have already gone a long way towards listening to the 'grass-roots' movement once again.

We are in the process of developing our own Centre for Excellence at the Uden Centre. Our enthusiasm is boundless but our sight is focused. It is, I feel, a project that Bill Uden would have valued and wanted for the staff and pupils of St Thomas the Apostle College as well as others who may wish to learn from our experiences.

Case Study 3
Learning Together: INSET in Networks (Holland)
Wiel Veugelers and Henk Zijlstra

This case study is condensed from Veugelers and Zijlstra (1995).

Context

The collaboration of schools in networks is increasingly regarded as an important means for the modernisation of education in the Netherlands. Since 1988 the Institute for In-Service Education of the University of Amsterdam has collaborated with 20 schools, under the name of School Network Upper Secondary Education HAVO/VWO (senior secondary education/pre-university education).

Schools learn from each other, analyse each other's practices and develop various initiatives. In-service educators, in their turn, stimulate and structure this interchange, and bring professionalism from outside the schools to the participating schools.

In Holland, upper secondary education consists of senior general education lasting two years (15–17), giving admission to higher vocational education and pre-university education lasting three years (15–18), giving admission to university study. Access to further and higher education is by passing the final examination, which is strictly controlled by the government, for the Diploma at the end of the course. Whereas upper secondary education tends to be driven by the need to gain the relevant Diploma, primary and lower secondary education is more child-centred, contains more cross-curriculum and extra-curriculum projects and is more orientated towards the development of social and learning skills. Also the development of values as part of citizenship education is more common in these phases of education.

In common with many countries around the world, upper secondary education in the Netherlands is currently subject to a government restructuring initiative, responding to changes in the student body (more independent and calculating) and the needs of the universities (a better preparation for higher level study). The Dutch education system allows each school, within the boundaries of government regulations and the National Curriculum, to organise its education in the way it prefers, and government policy is to increase this freedom of organisation through more financial autonomy, and more responsibility for differentiating the tasks of the staff and for the organisation and structuring of education. In return schools have, implicitly or explicitly, to account for their effectiveness, not only to the next level of education but also for the care of their students and for the cultural capital they wish to transfer to them.

The School Network Upper Secondary Education

Although the restructuring initiative is bringing greater uniformity to the curriculum, there cannot be just one answer for all schools. Each has to find its own solution to the various challenges. Institutes for In-service Education try to help schools meet the challenges by setting up contexts in which schools can learn from each other, not with the idea that solutions can be copied but because certain strategies, models and didactic methods can, in an adapted way, be used in the educational practice of individual schools and serve school development.

Relationships in the network

Participating in the network means contributing to a relaxed atmosphere, in which one can speak openly about one's school, in which there is respect for differences in views and practices. Ideas and products are used by referring to the people that develop them (more than 60 people participated in writing this case study). Also each school wants both to receive and to give, and everybody should be very sensitive in using information from other schools.

Functions of the network

In our experience we have distinguished five main functions of our network:

1 interpretation of government policies;
2 influencing government policies;
3 learning from each other's experience;
4 using each other's professionalism;
5 developing together a new education.

The following account of the development of the network addresses each of these functions.

Network phase 1 (1988–92)

The origins of the network were in a course provided by the Institute for In-service Education in response to a government plan to introduce a modular approach to upper secondary education. The participants told us that the course served the interests of schools by teaching them how to reflect on this segment of the education system. In a follow-up course we extended this practice of reflection on policy and educational practice and, although schools valued this opportunity, they also wished to discuss the problems they experienced in their own educational practice, how they analysed these experiences and what solutions they proposed.

The network that was subsequently set up involved upper secondary education co-ordinators, management staff and careers counsellors and also members of educational working groups or 'task forces'. Some of the schools have only one teacher participating in network meetings; other schools have three. There are two networks, each organising a minimum of six meetings a year.

From the moment schools join a network a substantial number of their staff regard their role in school not only as a teaching one but also as a tutoring one and wish to stimulate active learning. Staff members talk to each other about their educational practices with the staff participating in the network working not only on their own professional development but also on school improvement. The topics covered in network meetings during this period were the use of modular topics over a period of six weeks, learning skills in education (especially metacognitive skills through which pupils learn to analyse their own learning processes), the organisation and support system for the process of change in the context of restructuring, and topics related to tutoring, monitoring and counselling.

The restructuring we try to achieve takes place at the level of school organisation, curriculum, teaching and learning processes. Each school, based on its own view of education, has its own interpretation of the formal curriculum and its own tutoring system. In network meetings we try to explore these differences and use them in a productive way by enhancing the educational view that transcends these choices and, in particular, we try to see what this option means for the didactic methods used by the teachers.

The role of in-service educators

There are two in-service educators who are involved in all the meetings: one is recruited from the participating schools; the other, who is also the co-ordinator, is employed full-time at the university and combines in-service education and research. The in-service educators prepare and chair the meetings and facilitate the process of learning in the network both by holding sessions with members of the schools and by carrying out various activities in each school.

At regular times other in-service educators from the University of Amsterdam or teachers recruited from schools are involved in network meetings. The range of activities carried out involve consultancy, training courses, counselling of educational task forces, small research projects with teachers and discussion meetings with whole staff.

Sometimes the in-service educators participate in these activities; at other times they coach a number of people in the school in preparing and executing the activities. In their own schools network teachers operate as in-service educators and change agents.

Network phase 2 (1993–4)

The next stage in development of the network was to focus on three collectively selected themes and related work groups or 'task forces' to facilitate learning from participants' experience and using each other's professionalism. These were:

1 **Towards active learning.** This group involved 20 teachers from 15 schools and two in-service educators and covered related topics such as experimental learning and self-regulated learning. The concepts and practices were clarified with each participant describing their goal for the coming year and a route of activities designed to reach that goal. The participants worked as consultants to each other so each took home suggestions from other schools and in-service educators.

2 **Teaching time.** Various options for the length of teaching periods were explored by this group (e.g. 40/45, 60/65, 80 minutes) and also the potential for combinations of these.

3 **The third grade as the transition from lower to upper general education.** Sixteen teachers from 11 schools and two in-service educators participated in this group, starting with agreeing on ideal concepts for the curriculum within the government guidelines and then considering issues such as differentiation/homogeneity and the structure of the organisation of a model school which acted as a reference point for the plans of each participant school. The participants also worked as consultants to each other in this group and concluded their work by constructing a route of activities for the next year in each school and an activity plan for the group as a whole during the school year 1994–5.

Phase 3: Developing a new character to the Network (1994 on)

The network was relevant to schools not only because schools were implementing the outcomes of the shared consultancy but also because of the increased level of participation in activities outside their own schools. Arrangements had been made to free participants on Thursday afternoons to work together in the network and only five schools have withdrawn, two because of travelling distances, and two resulting from the network members being given other tasks in their schools. New schools joined to replace these so that the university's policy of investing in one network of 20 schools was maintained.

Each year the network had a meeting with a staff member from the Department of Education or an advisory committee for the restructuring of upper secondary education, making comments and suggestions on the operational issues arising from their plans. The opportunity was taken in these meetings to ask for resources to support networks, especially for the schools. This has resulted in the Steering Committee Upper Secondary Education allocating resources related to two developments: making new curricula and stimulating active learning in schools – though they speak of 'a place to study' rather than school. Indeed schools, are rethinking the teaching curriculum and developing the concept of 'student study loads', i.e. all the time a student has at her/his disposal for learning.

All in-service educators are paid from the budget Institutes for In-Service Education obtain from the government and now schools are also receiving delegated funds for INSET so they are able to contribute to network costs. They can also use the funds to buy INSET from other In-service Institutes. As a result, resources from the government are being used to accelerate activities at all levels in the network:

- all schools presently have a project team consisting of at least four people, of which one is a member of the school management;
- in their own schools, each school team does research, pilot projects, holds discussion meetings with the whole staff and makes a plan for the next few years;
- there are now six task forces;
- each school participates in at least three task forces;
- because of the resources obtained 'from the government', schools will be able to make their experiences and material transferable to other schools.

The six task forces are concerned with:

1 **Profiles:** the new curriculum, designed to reduce the huge variation in the combination of subjects, consists of a *common core* (45 per cent) of Dutch, two foreign languages, social studies, science and mathematics; *profiles* – these are 'science and technology', 'science and health',

'economics and society' and 'culture and society'; and an optional part of *free to choose* subjects.

2 **Active learning by introducing the study-load:** restructuring the organisation and didactic methods.

3 **Active learning by changing the curriculum:** the introduction of guide books for students.

4 **Learning and thinking skills for independent learning:** what does restructuring mean for the didactic methods used by teachers?

5 **Transition from lower to upper secondary education:** continuation and change in didactic methods, decision making, differentiation and homogeneity.

6 **Identity construction:** value education, citizen education and the hidden curriculum. What kind of pupil do we wish to create?

Many activities are planned at a level transcending the level of the individual schools. Regular network meetings take place six times a year, each of the six task forces has seven meetings and there will be five meetings with experts from outside the network who will not only give lectures but will also have a dialogue with the participants.

The character of the network is also changing because of the financial and political support given to the schools and In-Service Institutes in Holland by the government which is promoting the restructuring of education through the setting up of such development networks.

What has become clear is that networks have to be created, they cannot just be started by putting together a number of schools. Teachers and in-service educators need to learn to work together in a network, they need to feel comfortable in the group and they need to find out what they can offer and what they can receive. For teachers it is important that by building the network they can strengthen their position in the 'micro-politics' of the school, not for their own career but for enlarging the learning capacity of the school as an organisation.

Advantages for schools

The collaboration between schools within the network offers schools the following advantages:

- participants are given the chance to get acquainted with other organisational forms in education and with other ways of teaching;
- they see, and sometimes they even experience, that schools can always make other choices;
- they get to know the motives (educational views) lying behind these choices; and

- they can give some consideration to the way in which some (elements) of these views, educational organisations and didactic approaches could be used in their own school.

The school itself has to make explicit and clarify its own approach, and through the reactions of other schools and professionals the school obtains the necessary feedback for its further contribution to quality control.

Case Study 4
Managing Teacher Appraisal
Jeff Jones and Pauline Hughes

This case study is condensed from Hughes and Jones (1994).

Context

This school in this case study is situated in the town of Redditch, a mature 'new town' on the outskirts of Birmingham in the West Midlands. The borough is in the county of Hereford and Worcester, a rural county with a long tradition of working closely with its schools so that there have been very few opting for grant maintained status. The study concerns the collaboration between the school and the county's inspector for appraisal in the introduction of a consultative and collaborative approach to developing the skills for successful appraisal and integrating them into the normal practice of the school.

The principles of the Hereford and Worcester scheme for the introduction of appraisal were that:

- those presenting the scheme should have a commitment to the process and the credibility of teachers and headteachers;
- the arrangements for appraisal should be drawn up in full consultation with representatives of the professional associations and, where appropriate, with those of the Diocesan authorities;
- the scheme should be developmental, constructive and, wherever possible, positive;
- adequate training should be provided for all those involved in appraisal;
- the process should be two-way and related to the context of the school's and the appraisee's own stage of development.

Stages of introduction were:

1   What do teachers need to know about appraisal?

2 What do teachers need to feel about appraisal?

3 What do teachers need to be able to do within appraisal?

Collaboration between the LEA and its schools in bringing about the potential benefits of appraisal was seen as crucial. Team effort, involving the pooling and sharing of expertise and systematic reflection upon current practice, provides a valuable contribution to the management of initiatives such as appraisal.

Abbey High School: introducing appraisal

The principal purpose of introducing appraisal at the Abbey High School was, of course, to satisfy the statutory requirements laid down in the Teacher Appraisal Regulations and Circular 12/91. However, from the school's point of view, and from mine as the professional co-ordinator, it was vital that appraisal was introduced in the most positive way. In *Teaching Quality* (DES, 1983) it was stated that:

> ... *those responsible for managing the school teacher force have a clear responsibility to establish, in consultation with their teachers, a policy for staff deployment and training based on a systematic assessment of every teacher's performance, and related to their policy for the school curriculum.*

'... *In consultation with their teachers*' became the keynote of my task of implementing appraisal, although I would be the first to admit that there were occasions when consultation amounted to little more than persuading staff to accept the inevitable or explaining more fully some of the procedures involved.

The school's policy on appraisal was based on the Department for Education (DfE) Regulations and Circular, together with the LEA's guidelines. An early decision had been made by the head that the process of appraisal should be delegated to line managers rather than peers – certainly in the first instance. This would seem to be supported by Evans and Tomlinson (1989) who found that: 'The pilot studies ... lend weight to the case for senior managers, rather than peers as appraisers.' Although obliged to present this decision to the staff development committee (SDC) I felt it important to explain the decision by presenting the pros and cons of the various methods and allowing debate to take place. As a result it became the consensus view of the SDC that the 'line-manage' approach was preferable. Thus 'the conflict between bureaucracy and the claims of professional autonomy was accommodated ...' (Noble and Pym, 1970).

My belief was that the role of the SDC, an almost entirely democratically elected body, was crucial to the positive acceptance of a system of appraisal at the school. Perhaps more by accident than design, the committee reflects the bureaucratic structure of the school, but it is also constituted of those who carry the respect of the staff because of their individual strengths, of their competence as practitioners, and because of the sensitivity of their approach to sensitive issues; individually, they are also prepared to stand up and be counted!

The considerable work already done by this group on staff development made it possible for this initiative to be seen 'as an opportunity by which the individual and organisation can both benefit' (Fidler and Cooper, 1988). It was agreed unanimously that the appraisal system should be based on the developmental rather than the accountability model, and would be concerned with 'the improvements of practice by identifying strengths, weaknesses, needs and interests' (Turner and Clift, 1988).

The activities of this team reflected Handy's (1985) notion of a 'Task Culture' whose patron goddess is Athena. 'Athenian cultures tend to think of individuals as resourceful humans rather the human resources' and 'influence within this culture is based on expertise and the ability to get the job done'. I saw my role as managing the work of the team and promoting a team spirit. Strenuous efforts were made to promote a climate of trust to encourage the free expression of ideas, suggestions, doubts, reservations and fears. Because of the pressing nature of the initiative, it was essential that members of the group were clear about what needed to be done, the timescale involved and the nature of their individual responsibility.

Members of the SDC attended faculty meetings and listened to the concerns of staff. Problem questions were then referred to a full meeting of the SDC and members were able to discuss alternative approaches and solutions. One outcome was that I approached the head to seek a proviso that if an individual were unhappy about the designated appraiser, then the head should be prepared to allow an alternative if good grounds for such a change could be provided. This was accepted by the head.

The training for the SDC and the professional association representatives took place as planned and proved a valuable forum for debate. The disagreements over National Curriculum testing, the NUT Conference's opposition to appraisal and the reservations of the NAS/UWT to self-appraisal provided a dramatic backcloth to the day. It became apparent, however, that the LEA's stance was firmly supportive of the formative approach taken by the school, and equally the professional association was able to test the attitude of the head and SDC in the presence of the LEA's inspector for appraisal. Appraisal newsletters were also published at critical stages to limit, as far as possible, the 'distortion of information' (Handy, 1986) and to ensure that the purposes of appraisal were fully understood and agreed by all involved.

In turn the SDC – acting in pairs – trained members of the English, history, PE and science departments. Because of the relative lack of confidence of some less experienced members of the SDC, I felt that such an approach would play an important part in the development of the individual and heighten the profile of the team. Acting in an advisory capacity, I moved among the pilot groups expanding on the work of committee members. Each teacher was given exactly the same appraisal pack and identical training, in accordance with the declared policy. It was, however, interesting to note that not everyone interpreted the same information in the same way. On such occasions, it was prudent to allow other members of the pilot scheme to present their interpretation to the discordant voice, thus avoiding accusations of political manoeuvring by me.

The appraisal programme moved on apace during June and July because of the extra time created after the departure of Years 11 and 13. As with the best-laid plans, all did not go smoothly since some staff were also involved in programmes of training as mentors for initial teacher training; another member of staff suffered a serious illness. These instances alone had tremendous implications for the curriculum areas led by them, since they formed part of the pilot group. A compact was signed with Rover Group early in June, leading to an unexpected five-day absence for one of the SDC when he spent time at Longbridge.

Nevertheless, six of the original eight designated members of staff were fully appraised by the end of August (some report writing having been done during the holiday); four more experienced classroom observation, completed a self-appraisal form, had their appraisal discussion and were moving towards their agreed statement of achievements and targets. Appraisal targets were agreed with the first six appraisees and training evaluation sheets were received from 18. Structured semi-formal discussions have been conducted with members of the SDC and the six members of staff who have been completely appraised. Notes of questions raised at departmental meetings prior to SDC and pilot-group training were also logged.

Within the limited context of the training and the pilot scheme, the management of the introduction of appraisal would appear to have achieved its objectives. From the outset, the school's aim was to produce a scheme which would be formative, and hence be concerned with 'professional development, the improvement of practice by identifying strengths, weaknesses, needs and interests' (Jones, 1993). From this the quality of teaching and learning should be enhanced, and it would also satisfy managerial and accountability demands. Appraisal has to be seen as an integral part of a system of management, and, as such, is a part of 'a strategy for managing change and is linked with other aspects of institutional development' (Turner and Clift, 1988). It proved extremely difficult for me to be totally objective about my own role in the management of this initiative, but I was acutely aware that if a non-threatening climate were to be created then I would need to demonstrate 'integrity of character' (Drucker, 1988) and produce a scheme, which although in keeping with the bureaucratic demands of the DFE, LEA and the head, should also be seen as a two-way process, be the subject of negotiation and be flexible and multifaceted.

Case Study 5
Induction (Science Teachers in Israel)
Iris Geva-May and Yehudit Dori

This case study is condensed from Geva-May and Dori (1996).

Context

The Induction Project at the Technion, Israel Institute of Technology, began in the school year 1991–2. Although the project followed the policy guidelines and the goals set by the Israeli Ministry of Education, it was allowed academic and personal freedom in the design, as well as in the frequency and location of the meetings between the mentors and the new teachers. It differs from other existing induction models in that the graduating students are all teachers of science, mathematics and technology. These teachers teach in junior and high schools.

In the northern part of Israel, where the Technion serves as a teacher training site, there is a particular shortage of science and technology teachers. Moreover, the teacher population in this area is especially culturally diverse and includes minorities (Arab and Druze), former USSR immigrants and native Israeli teachers.

As a result, beginning science and technology teachers in the development towns of the north of the country might find that, in addition to the problems inherent in science education, they are also the only teachers in their specialisation area in their school. The lack of a senior colleague with the same disciplinary background who might have been of help in the absorption process adds another dimension to the difficulties with which the beginning teacher is confronted. Thus the special induction programme for beginning science and technology teachers needed to cover professional as well as organisational and emotional domains.

The Induction Project population

The project is aimed at beginning teachers who have graduated from the Department of Education in technology and science preceding their first year of teaching. There is an average of 50 teachers who graduate each year. The project is offered by the Technion and supported by the Israeli Ministry of Education, which supports similar activities in schools of education in other universities and colleges throughout the state.

The graduates are entitled to receive the services we offer on a voluntary basis. All graduating teachers have been sent letters of invitation to take part in this voluntary project. Each new teacher who responds positively is invited for a preliminary meeting with the mentors and the other peers.

In 1991, the first year of the project's operation, eight trainees were involved and three mentors in the subjects of chemistry, biology and electronics. In 1993, 16 beginning teachers, working in 12 different schools, took part in the project. They were instructed by six mentors in the subjects of chemistry, biology, mathematics, computer science and electronics. In 1994 the teacher population consists of 22 beginning teachers who were supported by ten mentors and the project director. We assume that the doubling of the number of teachers participating in the project is due to the dissemination of positive responses of the project's participants in the first year.

Objectives and characteristics of the Technion Teacher Induction Project

The objectives of this project are:

- to assist the beginning teachers in their integration process during their first year in school by providing assistance in both content knowledge, teaching methodologies and class management;
- to assist the beginning teachers to cope with the gap between their expectations and the school system by showing them ways that engender self-esteem, competence and collegiality;
- to diminish beginning teachers' drop-out, which is sometimes more severe for teachers of high potential who are more vulnerable to extreme class situations;
- to improve communication between teachers and their school system: principal, area co-ordinators, counsellors and parents.

The Technion Teacher Induction Project is characterised by a number of features as shown in Figure 8.1.

The mentors meet with their trainees once a week over a period of one school year. They help the trainees in designing lesson plans, class management, efficient time utilisation, homework planning and personal

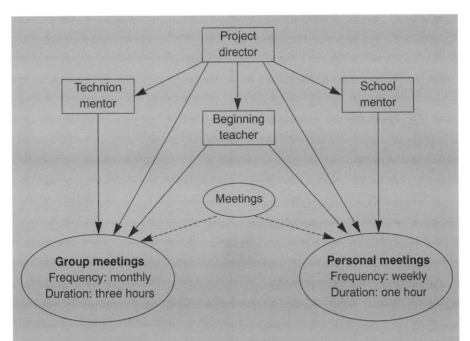

Figure 8.1: The Technion Induction Project infrastructure

intercommunication with the administration, area co-ordinator and peer teachers. This informal framework enables positive co-operation between the mentor and the beginning teacher and provides the teacher with moral support.

The project director keeps in constant contact with the mentors and a number of the trainees to ensure that a good rapport exists between each mentor–teacher pair and to minimise drop-outs from the project. Each year only one or two of the new teachers do not make it to the end of the school year because of maternity leave or extensive workload.

During the school year, monthly meetings for the entire group are organised. In these meetings all the participants share ideas and experiences and suggest ways to improve the induction project's effectiveness. Some of the meetings are devoted to a specific topic related to teaching in general, and teaching science and technology in particular. Examples of such topics include: integrating environmental education into the science curriculum; improving the use of models, computer-assisted instruction modules (CAI) (Dori, 1995) and demonstrations to increase students' motivation; fostering students' high-level cognitive skills; and using alternative evaluation tools.

Evaluation of the Technion Teacher Induction Project

The evaluation model adopted followed the type of feedback required by the decision makers and was based on the model set up by the Phi-Delta-Kappa Committee (Stufflebeam *et al.*, 1971). It consisted of three stages: identification of information needs, collection of data, analysis and provision of the collected data to decision makers. The role of the evaluation was viewed as formative (Scriven, 1967; Stufflebeam *et al.*, 1971; Chelimsky, 1985) and the evaluation questions decided upon served the formative information needs of these decision makers. The questions were concerned with three main areas of concern: professional development of the beginning teachers, relationships between the new teachers and their mentors, and the impact of the project on the new teacher's work in his/her first year of teaching.

Therefore, the evaluation questions addressed were related to the impact of the programme on the development of communication skills, class-management skills, teaching skills, role awareness and satisfactory mentor–teacher interaction. Each evaluation question was represented by a series of questionnaire statements forming an evaluation cluster. The respondents were required to react to these statements on a four-point Likert scale: strongly agree, agree, disagree and strongly disagree. The average ratings of all the statements was represented on evaluation cluster points at the tendency of the attitude and to the strength of that tendency.

Summary and conclusions

The induction policy in Israel has started to take off towards the end of the 1980s and, currently, its implementation is at an advanced stage, but it is not compulsory. The Technion Induction Programme presented in this section is unique in that it is aimed at serving new science and technology teachers who have recently graduated from the Department of Education in Technology and Science. By following the induction policy guidelines the Technion Induction Project has been instrumental in alleviating the special obstacles new science teachers face during their first school year, and has contributed to increased teacher motivation and performance. We define the principles of the induction policy in Israel, present a model that combines these principles with science and technology teaching principles, and discuss the findings of evaluation research regarding the project's conduct and outcomes to date.

The contribution of the induction project to the beginning teachers is multifaceted and relates to the following issues:

- discussing and solving professional problems concerning issues such as the school system and class composition;

- helping to cope with class management problems;
- providing moral support during the initial absorption stage, including strengthening self-confidence and status in the class;
- discussing and solving professional problems concerning the subject matter, e.g. design of lesson plans, laboratories and tests, and the use of models and CAI modules;
- improving the status of the science subject in the school, in particular if the beginning teacher is the first to teach the subject in the school;
- helping to implement various science teaching strategies and teaching modes and adapting them to the different class types;
- helping to deal with students who are in need of special education although officially they are not classified as such.

Overall, the Technion induction/support project can be considered successful: it has been instrumental in alleviating the difficulties and fears new science teachers face during their first school year, and has catered for self-confidence and a better orientated state of mind. The drop-out rate was reduced to only one from the induction group in the year reported in this study. At the end of the following three academic years no drop-outs have been reported.

The achievements obtained showed that this induction project has fulfilled the induction policy goals set up by the Ministry of Education as regards helping the beginning teachers in the first, most difficult year, encouraging pre-service teachers to start teaching, prevent drop-out and improving the pre-service training by applying feedback from the induction process (Mor, 1989). Moreover, the project has been particularly instrumental in schools in which there was no senior staff to support the beginning teacher or in which a particular science and technology discipline (such as chemistry and computer science) had not been taught at all due to the lack of a teacher in this discipline.

In subsequent years the project has been expanded in both magnitude and methodology, and has put more emphasis on role definition, on teaching skills within the new teacher's domain and on emotional needs. Future expansion of the Technion Induction Project is planned in order to help as many beginning teachers as possible who will benefit from proper induction, the principles of which have been developed and confirmed in this study.

Conclusion to the case studies

We hope you enjoyed reading about these experiences of organising innovative professional development in schools and are sufficiently motivated to begin, continue or evaluate your own projects. Whatever your own context, we suggest the common features of these examples is that they paid attention to the essentials and kept a focus on achievement while supporting the people involved in the project. What we also believe to be significant is that they evaluated their success and took the trouble either to write it up themselves or to get someone connected with the project to do so. The recording of learning forms the important function of objectifying it and giving it an external reality which can then be judged against the original aims and other examples of similar initiatives.

Having given some exemplars of what some people are doing in the field, in Part III we want to push the boundaries of thinking about both corporate and individual professional development in the context of the emerging understanding of management and leadership, both in schools and in the wider environment of business and society.

PART THREE

∎ ∎ ∎

Creating a Learning Community

9

■ ■ ■

Building the Learning Leader for the Learning Organisation

This chapter draws together the threads of the previous sections of the book and looks at the characteristics of leaders of the future and the types of organisations they lead.

Capturing corporate learning

The key concepts we have been outlining in this book concern developing a dynamic balance between achieving synergy from aligning individual and corporate learning so that their different elements fit together and are cohesive while, at the same time, injecting energy into the system through challenge, distributed power, leadership and team building.

This dynamic balance is not easy to achieve as there is no known way of maintaining a perfect status quo, even in systems which are well understood. There is always an element of what engineers call 'hunting' – that is the effect of feedback in a system over- or under-compensating for change. The easiest example to take to illustrate this is the operation of a thermostat in a central heating system. As the water in the system cools, the temperature sensor will detect a drop in air temperature until it reaches its 'switch on' point and activates the circulation pump (and through further feedback sensors in the boiler turns on the heating). The water in the radiators will then heat up and raise the air temperature until the room thermostat detects that the room temperature has reached the desired level as set by the occupant. However, the hot water in the radiators will continue to heat the room and raise the temperature so there will be an 'overshoot'. As a result the room temperature will always be several degrees too hot or too cold, although these extremes will tend to get closer together the longer the heating has been operating.

You can see a similar effect of over- and under-shooting when a baby learns to pick up a toy. As her arm reaches out for the toy, her hand will swing wildly over the object but with an ever decreasing arc until the baby feels she is near enough to make a grab. The mechanism is very similar to the example described above – again, as the baby becomes more experienced the 'hunting' or wild swinging either side of the object will be much less extreme as she learns finer and finer control over the feedback mechanisms through her hand–eye co-ordination and kinaesthetic sense of where her hand is in relation to the toy.

In studying such mechanisms from a systems approach we are learning much more about the energy inputs and regulatory feedback systems in human and physical relationships. If you watch predatory animals and birds when they are hunting (for example, cats and hawks) you will see them deliberately putting extra energy into their head movements in order to track their prey more accurately. Increasing the swing and field of view enables them to make a more accurate strike. Similarly, you will see a shuffling movement of the rear quarters of cats as they are about to strike as it is easier to get up to full speed if their body is moving than if it is completely still – even though the movement might mean they are detected earlier by their prey.

So how can our growing understanding of such feedback mechanisms in learning be applied to the tricky business of responding to change while establishing confidence and expertise in the team members and leadership? Put at its simplest, we need to understand the process (or the system itself) as well as the roles of the individuals in the process. However, in human systems we also have issues of motivation, negotiation, communication, perception and power (in the political sense) to add into the equation. All too often, management and administration approaches reduce problematic issues to matters of simplistic rational strategic planning, even though the original impetus may have come from wide left field through intuition, vision, foresight, wisdom or other such key attributes of successful leadership.

The net effect of over-reliance on rational/logical feedback approaches in human systems is to attempt to restore stability by a reduction of the energy input to the 'hunting' mechanism described above and thus to dampen the system swings. It is true that this can work in the short term very successfully but it does also reduce the system's ability to respond to environmental turbulence caused by exponential increases in the rate of change. Let us take two examples.

The Teacher Training Agency has developed a framework for continuing professional development covering the stages between initial teacher training up to long-serving headteachers (TTA, 1996). The framework itself is still being mapped out and therefore a deal of 'hunting' is evident – the tension between the original suggestions for 'Expert Teacher' competencies and the notion of the 'Advanced Skills Teacher' in the White Paper (*Excellence in Education*, 1997) is an illustration. This puts extra energy into the system and enables it to ride the turbulence of changing and developing thinking, both from those in power and those in the profession who have the day-to-day knowledge of teaching and learning practice. On the other hand, the competencies for the National Professional Qualification for Headship (thought up by a very experienced education adviser seconded to the TTA and developed through wide consultation – taking advantage of the extra energy available through the process of 'hunting') have been codified and standardised nationwide through committee and will be delivered by pre-programmed methods of training using a common package of materials. This is taking energy out of the system, damping down the hunting effect and ossifying a collaborative learning process into one of the knowledge transfer of received wisdom.

The second example concerns approaches to school improvement through target setting and monitoring through numerical performance indicators. There is a good head of steam being built up over this through a number of initiatives such as the GEST School Improvement project, the Year 11 Information System (YELLIS) and A-Level Information System (ALIS) – both from the CEM Centre, University of Durham – approaches to upper secondary school performance improvement and the use of OFSTED indicators in the Pre-Inspection Contextual and School Indicators (PICSI) reports provided at the initial stages of a school inspection. Of course, the use of performance indicators, careful monitoring and benchmarking does a great deal to create the data-rich context which is characteristic of successful school improvement. However, the creation of this data-rich context is a necessary but not sufficient attribute – what is done with and as a result of the data is the more important side of the equation. Thus we are, at the moment, injecting much energy into the system hunting for appropriate indicators and suitable methods of analysis and as a result there is evidence of performance improvement. The danger is that certain standard measures will be adopted as a proxy for measuring the channelling of this energy and the system will decay to a lowest common denominator (we are two points above our competitors so we are OK) instead of seeking the highest common factor by continuing the hunting process (search for the best and find out what they do).

What can school leaders do in practical terms to maintain the energy in the system and ensure it is directed towards sustaining improvement? It is the assertion in this book that the one single sufficient condition for this to occur is a focus on learning at the individual, team and school-wide levels. Of course, this does not mean that developing, recording and reviewing performance does not mean generating and analysing appropriate data but that, without a focus on what this means for learning at all levels, the system will cease to 'hunt' and will decay. As an analogy, we would like to introduce the notion of 'innovation half-life'.

We have seen a vast number of educational (and some not so educational!) initiatives flowing through schools in the last decade, each of which is introduced with a flurry of activity, creating tension and conflict (which can be read as energy), taking a number of years to reach acceptance (or acquiescence) – the 'half-life' – after which there is a rapid decay in the amount of energy. Appraisal is but one example of this. Indeed, the waste output of this educational initiative has been recycled several times and its half-life extended when perhaps the original issues of performance review and professional development could have been more effectively tackled head-on and the energy used to develop new approaches which could become part of the system's capacity for self-renewal. Indeed, many successful schools and authorities have done just this!

The task, therefore, is to identify the key factors which will assist leaders in directing the energy created in the initial 'half-life' of educational change and then to make sure that the system learns so that the knowledge achieved, often painfully, becomes part of the stock in trade of the school and remains accessible and useful. In setting up ways of dealing with this we need to focus on:

- **People:** individually, one-on-one and in groups.
- **Process:** understanding the system and maintaining the energy flow.
- **Policy:** agreeing core values, producing a statement and relating action to this.

For the people in the organisation (and in schools we must stress that this needs to be *all* the people – students, teachers, support staff, visiting professionals as well as parents and the work and social community) the mind-set of a learning community needs to be developed. Strategies for encouraging individual learning are covered later in this chapter but opportunities must also be sought for learning when in a one-on-one situation. A large number of encounters between leaders and team members consist of these type of situations – often very brief meetings snatched in breaks and between lessons as well as more formal appointments – and a focus on knowledge capture and learning would maximise and direct the energy rather than let it dissipate as heat and tension. Michael Barber (1997) says we should change our greetings from 'What do you do?' and 'How are you?' to 'What are you learning?' in order to focus more on the core task in schools and society.

In terms of understanding the system we need to build a picture of the learning process which combines left-brain activities such as logical thinking, analysis and rationality with our developing understanding of right-brain aspects such as intuition, emotional and social skills, wisdom and judgement (see Figure 9.1).

In seeking to work with the organisation's learning system we must pay particular attention to the feedback loops which characterise a learning organisation. It is these which enable the system both to expend energy in monitoring the environment in hunting for alternative solutions and to operationalise them in the context of the organisation.

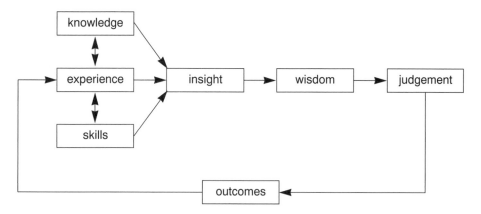

Figure 9.1: A whole brain approach to learning systems

In Chapter 2 mention was made of Swieringa and Wierdsma's (1992) notion of the use of the learning cycle approach in creating a learning organisation which may be illustrated as in Figure 9.2.

The feedback loops here operate at increasingly deeper levels of learning so that the organisation monitors its learning in terms of not only the surface level of adjustments to the rules which govern behaviour and get results but also the more profound levels of the principles and insights which arise from the core values and mission of the organisation.

Such a perception of the school operating as a learning system needs to be underpinned by the way in which individuals and groups pay attention to the creation and recording of knowledge. In the wider world of industry and commerce it has become a truism that people are an organisation's greatest asset, in particular their knowledge. One of the downsides to reengineering, downsizing, delayering and restructuring has been the bleeding away of longer-serving middle and senior managers – those who have lived through

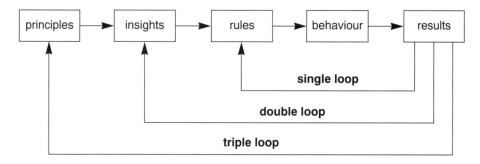

Figure 9.2: Organisational learning loops
Source: Swieringa and Wierdsma, 1992. Reprinted by permission of Addison Wesley Longman Ltd.

more than one cycle of economic activity. Such persons have a wealth of knowledge about how the organisation coped with the cycle before the one it is currently in but when they leave through redundancy or early retirement they take their knowledge (knowledge of *and* knowledge how) with them, sometimes using it to their personal advantage in consultancy, possibly to your competitors!

So valuable is this knowledge and so serious the issue that the term 'corporate amnesia' has now come into management-speak to describe the phenomenon. Perhaps the opposite of a learning organisation is a forgetting or amnesiac one! Indeed, a number of companies in the USA now make their living from being knowledge management consultants and advising organisations on how to capture such important information through regular 'knowledge identification' sessions leading to archiving outcomes and the processes used to achieve them. This is moving a long way beyond the notion of an 'exit interview' which many companies are now conducting as a regular feature of their procedures when individuals leave the organisation. Unless the company has a strategy for capturing knowledge, storing it so it is readily accessible to managers and their teams and making it a priority to consult such records (and persons who lived through the process in question), people leaving the company are hardly likely to be in an appropriate mood to share their knowledge and experience when their minds are on the move and their next job (or indeed retirement). We have direct experience of an LEA which made available a counsellor for those taking early retirement or being made redundant and then made that person redundant – which didn't exactly put him in the best frame of mind to help others or feed the experience of those leaving back into the reorganisation!

If the notion of knowledge management is now seen as so important, how much more so should be the concept of learning management – or, to align this idea with the major premise of this book – learning leadership. There are a number of key strategies which schools could use to achieve a focus on learning at all levels, involving individual, one-on-one and group learning and enabling both surface learning and deep/profound learning. These involve looking for obvious solutions such as creating records and archives of plans, monitoring information and outcomes, but also remembering that the most significant information may well be in the collective memories of the staff as they attempted to create meaning out of the contexts in which they found themselves. School leaders can no doubt extend the following list from their own experience when considering the most effective way of leading, learning and capturing systemic knowledge in their schools:

1 **Learning relationships:** identifying individual learning styles in both staff and pupils.
2 **Learning partners:** informal arrangements between staff (and students) to identify, record and review 'knowledge of' (facts and terms) and 'knowledge how' (skills and processes).

3 **Learning contracts:** more formal agreements, linked to professional development for staff and individual action plans for students.

4 **Process reviewers:** appointing a member of the team to feed back on the process of development.

5 **Whole team and school review:** periodic review of the learning strategies and outcomes both within teams and across the school.

6 **Value-auditing decisions:** reviewing policies and previous decisions against the present statement of core values – and recording the value statements which lie behind current decisions for future reference!

Such an agenda can appear very daunting as one rarely knows which data will turn into information which is useful for decision making, let alone which collection of knowledge will result in learning and thus carry meaning into the future. However, the penalty for *not* paying attention to learning through the school is to risk learning slower than the rate of change and letting the pupil and staff experience decay and stagnate. We are never likely to see the whole picture and therefore be able to pick out just the relevant parts, but we can use what we know now to take some snapshots which will tell us where we have been and help us to prepare for the uncertain future that lies ahead.

To illustrate how this might feel, I am reminded of an incident which happened to myself and a friend in the summer we left college. We were touring Scotland and 'doing the sights'. As geographers, we were passionate about landscape – especially the lumpy bits which you get *par excellence* in western Scotland – so we determined to climb Ben Nevis. My friend was a PE man so no going up the easy route for us (I knew there was an easy route as my father had driven most of the way up the mountain in a jeep on manoeuvres in the army), so we parked at the foot of the south face and started up the steep bit. Both of us were veterans of many a field trip so we had good boots, warm clothes, cagoules, food and water and the confidence of youth. Everything seemed so straightforward – we could almost see the top glinting in the sunshine and could imagine ourselves there, eating our sandwiches and drinking a well earned beer.

After about an hour of climbing, we found ourselves on an increasingly steep and slippery scree slope. The bright sunshine had turned to an overcast, wet, low cloud and the top of the mountain was now lost from sight, but we had been in worse situations than this so we carried on – hardly noticing that our route down had also disappeared from view. After another half an hour or so the weather had really closed in. We could no longer see the traverse we were aiming for and we were enveloped in a wet, clinging mist of low cloud which was making the scree very slippery. Both of us had enjoyed scree walking in Wales (when no one considered it environmentally damaging) so we knew that once the rock slope started moving, down was the only way to go. But we had traversed quite a way across the mountain looking for a route up the east side and had lost track of what the terrain looked like directly below us.

We were in quite a serious position. Our mental map of where we had come from was distorted (we had not thought to take bearings and record what we knew about the ground we had covered) and we could not see more than a few yards ahead. We hadn't taken note of the weather forecast and so could be locked into the fog for quite some time. On top of this my friend was getting cold and panicky – he was all for going back down immediately but what about that scree slope? Once the rocks started moving we could only traverse across the slope, we could not stop – and there may well be a precipice below us for all we knew. Instinctively I knew that we had to go up – all upward directions led to the top and we could come down the wide track my father had driven up so long ago. My friend took a deal of persuading, though; his emotions had taken over and he wasn't thinking rationally – all he wanted to do was get down and out of there, even if it meant going over a cliff.

The day was saved when we agreed to go on up for a few minutes and see whether we could get off the scree. Looming out of the mist was a scaffold pole – at least somebody else had been here. As we reached the pole we looked up the mountain and could just see another pole about fifty yards away. Could this be coincidence, we thought, or were we onto something at last? Up we went to the next pole. The terrain was still just as dodgy and the mist glowering but when we arrived at the next pole we could clearly see another one further on – and the one we had just come from was also just discernible through the fog. The mental map began to be reformed. We never did see any more than three poles at a time but we could visualise the ground we had covered and our confidence began to return – people had travelled this way before!

Eventually, with a great deal of relief, we reached the top to be confronted by a notice at the foot of the top pole which said 'Dangerous Route – experienced rock climbers only'. However, our mental map was now complete. We knew where we had come from – and had no wish to test out our experience as rock climbers by going back down the poles, though I think we could have done that if there was no other way. Ahead of us was the broad flat expanse at the top of the mountain where we could battle with the inevitable sheep to see who would eat our sandwiches first – there was even some snow lying in the dip at the north face to prove we had achieved something worth doing. The fog had lifted a bit and, on the way down the jeep track, we were treated to occasional glimpses of the range and the tarn so I now feel I have quite a good picture of what Ben Nevis looks like. The trip down and back up the road to the car was uneventful and we soon forgot how we felt stranded on the south slope of the highest mountain in Britain – but it is a lesson I will never forget, both in terms of using rationality and intuition to find a solution to a crisis and in taking responsibility for leading fellow human beings who may be temporarily out of their minds.

Leading a learning organisation is a little like climbing Ben Nevis in the fog – when you are stuck halfway up a mountain and can't see the way ahead, you need to have a good mental map of where you have come from, some accurate data about your last position and what is likely to happen in the immediate future, the confidence to think through the options and then to choose the most likely route to success using all your experience, wisdom and judgement. Once you have chosen your route, make sure you continue to record your progress and review the options as they arise – it is never going to get any clearer than that!

In applying such thinking to life in schools, perhaps the most important aspects to pay attention to are the way in which the groups and teams in the school work and how the leadership function is aligned and distributed through the organisation. Gareth Morgan (1986) gives us an insight into the way teams need to operate in learning organisations:

1 **Requisite variety:** within each team there needs to be a range of experience and skills to enable the team to respond to short- and long-term changes in context.

2 **Redundancy of functions:** redundancy here means spare capacity, to ensure the team is able to adapt to and take advantage of future market needs. If there is no spare capacity, flexibility of response to changes in the environment is reduced.

3 **Minimum critical specification:** those nearest the customer (class teachers) are those best equipped to identify shifts in strategic direction, so management needs to set the broad general parameters (strategic intent) and let the team work out the specifics in practice.

4 **Team learning:** if the organisation works on these principles, the team needs to develop strategies to enhance individual and team learning and to record and archive results for future use.

Morgan refers to an organisation working on these principles as a 'holographic' organisation, i.e. any part of the organisation has the same culture, ways of working and characteristics as the whole organisation. If you chop off a small part of a hologram you still get the whole picture but a smaller version; if you cut off part of a photograph, you don't get the whole picture.

Such an organisation is better able to respond to change through its distributed capacity to learn; as a result the leadership needs to recognise this and operate more flexibly: White *et al.* (1996) examine the key characteristics of such an approach to leadership in the twenty-first century and conclude that the core skills of successful leaders need to be:

1 **Difficult learning.** Leaders need to develop the capacity to reframe and restructure their models of how the world works. This means achieving 'deep learning', not just incremental adjustments to what has previously been learnt.

2 **Maximising energy.** Modern organisations are in a constant state of turbulence and turmoil, reflecting the pace of change in the external environment. The leader needs to support the creation of this energy and seek to align the conflicting forces through achieving synergy.

3 **Resonant simplicity.** Complexity on the surface needs to be balanced by an underlying simplicity of vision. The leader should maintain and develop the vision and seek to align motivation throughout the organisation.

4 **Multiple focus.** In order to push the achievement of the vision out to all parts of the organisation, the staff need to be advancing on all fronts.

5 **Mastering inner sense.** Finally leaders need to be confident in their mental maps of their environment through both personal mastery and being in tune with the waves of history.

A leader in such an organisation needs to develop, maintain and articulate a strong sense of personal and professional values as this provides the foundation upon which a responsive and learning organisation can be built. However, although we have been referring in this passage to 'the leader', this does not mean that there is only one leader or that leadership is restricted to middle and senior management. In an organisation that is successfully responding to and taking advantage of rapid change, leadership needs to be distributed through all levels – this also means that the organisation's core values need to be lived out through the leaders at all levels.

The next section will focus on how leaders in schools can develop this 'inner sense' so that there is both an alignment of insights and principles and requisite variety and challenge to keep the school moving forward.

Central to this book has been the proposition that leadership and learning are in a symbiotic relationship. One is not possible without the other and the success of one is determined by the extent to which the other is available. Of course it is perfectly possible for schools to function in the absence of one or both. Indeed we would argue that schools which are regarded as failing, not successful or of limited effectiveness have no access to the related concepts of leadership and learning. Many schools which are perceived to be reasonably effective may well be dominated by management and teaching rather than leadership and learning.

This distinction is not purely semantic. In differentiating between leadership and management and learning and teaching there are fundamental and profound issues in terms of perceived purpose, values, culture and hence what are perceived to be valid and significant activities. It is therefore essential to distinguish between leadership and management and learning and the outcomes of teaching.

The relationship between these elements is shown in Figure 9.3 which distinguishes between leadership and management, and profound and shallow learning.

It follows from this model that leadership and profound learning are about the individual's response to complexity expressed through a range of activities which are personal and related to higher-order and significant outcomes. Managing and shallow learning are not necessarily 'wrong' but are inevitably inhibited in their potential to support individual and organisational growth.

LEADING	PROFOUND LEARNING
Understanding complexity	Recognising variables
Focus on core purpose	Focus on learning
Development through relationships	Learning partnerships
Emphasis on processes	Individual activity
Creating the capacity to act	Implementation and application
Creating Wisdom	
MANAGING	SHALLOW LEARNING
Implementation	Replication
Consistency	'Right' answers
Structures	Generic activities
Control	Passivity
Linearity	Chronological progression
Predictability	Imposed assessment
Ensuring Conformity	

Figure 9.3: Leading and profound learning, managing and shallow learning

Both are essentially subordinate activities – legitimated by the requirements of most educational systems but profoundly limiting and a denial of potential.

The synthesising feature of leadership and profound learning is the creation of wisdom by the individual. According to Csikszentmihalyi and Rathorde (1990) wisdom has three distinguishing dimensions:

1. *[It] refers to attempts at understanding the world in a disinterested way, seeking the ultimate consequences of events as well as ultimate causes while preserving the integration of knowledge. (p. 48)*

2. *Wisdom is a virtue because by relating in a disinterested way the broadest specimen of knowledge, it provides the most compelling guide to action . . . Only a truly disinterested, long-range, organic understanding of consequences can pull us back from the brink of disaster. (pp. 48–9)*

3. *Finally, wisdom is a personal good, an intrinsically rewarding experience that provides some of the highest enjoyment and happiness available. (p. 49)*

This combination of the cognitive, moral and personal provides a powerful model of the nature and purpose of leadership and learning. In the context of the school it is vital that it is led, in all its dimensions, by people who are aware of all three elements. It is only through such leadership that learners will be able to develop wisdom in their own lives. Burns (1978) expresses this approach using Maslow's concept of self-actualisation – the highest order human activity:

> *I suggest that the most marked characteristic of self-actualisers as potential leaders ... is their capacity to learn from others and the environment – the capacity to be taught ...*

> *It is this kind of self-actualisation that enables leaders to comprehend the needs of potential followers, to enter into their perspectives ... Because leaders themselves are continually going through self-actualisation processes, they are able to rise with their followers ... to respond to their transformed needs and thus help followers more into self-actualisation processes. (p. 117)*

Thus the leader is model, learner and facilitator, each component being necessary to increase confidence that learning is both the process and the outcome. This approach also raises the fundamentally important issue that leadership is situational – it is necessary for the whole school, for each constituent team, in every classroom and in every project and process. This challenges any notion of leadership as the occupation of a position of hierarchically determined status. It is rather a relationship which is founded on the capacity to learn and to facilitate learning.

Of course it is perfectly possible to justify a well managed school – it will undoubtedly give 'value for money' and meet, or surpass, the prevailing criteria for public accountability. However, this is to ignore the issues that were raised in Chapter 1 and in particular Stoll and Fink's (1996) powerful insight that 'Many of our schools are good schools if this were 1965' (p. 1). They go on to differentiate between schools which are sinking, struggling, strolling, cruising or moving. It is only the moving schools that

> *... are not only effective in 'value added' terms but people within them are also actively working together to respond to their changing context and to keep developing. They know where they are going; they have systems and the 'will and the skill' to get there. (p. 86)*

Barber (1997) reinforces this point:

> *The teaching profession cannot rebuild its sense of purpose and self-respect by hankering after the past. It needs – soon – to begin to think about the world that is coming and to prepare itself for the immense challenges ahead. The learning society cries out for the leadership of a learning profession. (p. 238)*

This implies a profession that understands leadership, is capable of learning and, most importantly, can reconcile the two in principle and practice. What is not needed to support this change is a list of mechanistic, instrumental and reductionist competencies. Rather there is a need to create a vocabulary of understanding which allows individuals to develop a response within a redefined culture and set of expectations. Professional learning which focuses on leadership qualities has to take place within a context of new semantics. It has been argued throughout this book that leadership and learning are axiomatic – nobody ever learnt by being managed, no school has ever improved by being well managed.

In the final analysis the qualities of leaders and learners are the same. In his study *What Makes A Good Teacher*, Hare (1993) identifies a range of qualities which, he argues, are a necessary response to increasingly reductionist approaches:

> *Too much attention in teacher education continues to be placed on the role and routine, on particular techniques which research is supposed to have deemed effective in promoting learning. This is partly because we are afraid to use our judgement in selecting and approving those who have desirable intellectual, moral and personal qualities and so we fall back on observable and measurable behaviours; and partly because we work with an impoverished concept of education itself which continues to be seen as nothing more than the acquisition of information and skills. (pp. iv–v)*

Hare identifies eight qualities central to the notion of the 'good teacher' – humility, courage, impartiality, open-mindedness, empathy, enthusiasm, judgement and imagination. It does not take a major intellectual leap, nor does it involve a distortion of Hare's argument, to transpose the qualities of the teacher into those of the leader and learner. An explanation of each of the qualities will demonstrate the parallels.

Humility is a necessary precondition to both leading and learning in that there has to be a deference and respect of the status and dignity of others and just how much one does not know. Humility is the necessary antidote to power derived from status, from an (understandable) justification of experience and the psychologically inevitable commitment to one's own values and world-view. For the leader and teacher failure to apply the antidote results in an unjustified confidence in the rightness of a particular stance. The learner needs humility to be receptive, to recognise the power of other ideas and the possibility that there are multiple perspectives and no right answers.

Courage relates to the willingness of leader and learner to admit ignorance and failure, to accept that they might be viewed by others as something less than perfect. It also refers to moral courage – to express through their actions fundamental principles and beliefs and to use their leadership and learning to espouse and support certain key ethical propositions.

Impartiality is one of the defining features of both the effective learner and leader in the sense of recognising and dealing with personal bias in working with others and actively combating bias through the use of evidence, debate and argument. Leadership in particular offers abundant opportunities to further bias, especially in the classroom. Learning no less is inevitably circumscribed by unrecognised or unacknowledged bias. An essential element of professional learning is the development of skills of reasoning, analysis and argument.

Open-mindedness develops out of impartiality and is characterised by a receptiveness to alternative perspectives and, in particular, a willingness to follow an argument through to its logical conclusion. For leaders and learners this raises the challenge of being open to alternative models, theoretical constructs, evidence and the translation of theory into practice. One of the defining differences between leadership and management and shallow and profound learning is the willingness to respond to new, challenging and alternative stimuli.

Empathy is best characterised as genuineness in response to others. This has long been argued as an essential prerequisite of leadership, as part of the essential portfolio of attitudes which allows for genuine relationships with others. As was demonstrated in Chapters 3 and 4, the basis of professional learning is to be found in relationships. Caring for and about others as leader, learner or teacher is about recognition, respect and involvement. All effective leading and learning relationships are founded on trust which in turn is a product of mutual regard and respect. The precise nature of such relationships will inevitably alter according to role, age, etc. but the fundamental principle as encapsulated by Covey (1989) remains: 'Understand in order to be understood.'

Enthusiasm is perhaps the most contentious of Hare's maxims – it is not easily prescribed in an era of cynicism, criticism and formal accountability. Yet it remains a powerful, transformative force in leading, learning and teaching. To lead and to learn as opposed to manage and be taught requires elements such as love, passion, involvement and even a degree of obsession. This is found in the best of leaders, learners and teachers and it is contagious and transformational. The positive sense of self and attitude towards what has to be done, which are the most direct expressions of enthusiasm, are essential corollaries of leading and learning. Both are potentially too difficult and too fraught with the potential for failure to be engendered through polite interest, cautious acceptance or a diffident involvement.

Judgement can be seen as the most significant outcome of professional learning and the pivotal activity of leadership. As Figure 9.1 shows, the generation of wisdom is the essential precursor to judgement and the criterion for both effective learning and leadership is the capacity to demonstrate judgement. Sound judgement is often perceived as the definition of an educated person. As Hare puts it:

> *In this way, the development of judgement includes a necessary familiarity with the information and ideas on which we draw in framing our own views, but also a critical distance from what we are learning so that we can assess these ideas, discarding, modifying and applying them as appropriate. (p. 133)*

Although the judgements of the leader of an organisation might be seen to have wider implications and broader significance than those of the individual learner, the processes are essentially the same.

Imagination is fundamental to leaders and learners, especially in complex times. Change, innovation and development all require insight which draws on new perspectives. Creativity is one of the hallmarks of valid leadership and learning – whether generating new strategies for the organisation or new insights into a classic academic problem. Indeed leadership is often seen in terms of the ability to reorder and to introduce better ways. The more complex the problem the less likely it is to be solved by management strategies or didactic approaches. The most dynamic leaders and learners are practitioners of intellectual artistry and creativity and professional learning can only be vindicated by the extent to which imagination is allowed to flourish in the creation of new responses, ideas and insights.

It is perhaps appropriate to end this book, which has sought to draw parallels between leading and learning, with quotations from people who combined leadership with learning and teaching. Illich (1971) argued:

> *As citizens have new choices, new chances for learning, their willingness to seek leadership should increase. We may expect that they will experience more deeply both their own independence and their need for guidance. As they are liberated from manipulation by others, they should learn to profit from the discipline others have acquired in a lifetime. Deschooling education should increase – rather than stifle – the search for men with practical wisdom who would be willing to sustain the newcomer in his educational adventure. As masters of their art abandon the claim to be superior, infamous or skill models, their claim to superior wisdom will begin to ring true. (pp. 98–9)*

If we set aside Illich's masculine language, we see he is describing the process of learning and leadership being integrated into a common pursuit of personal and social growth.

In his discussion of Paulo Friere's critical pedagogy Shor (1993) raises the issue of the appropriate conceptual framework for teachers working in a democratic way to challenge inequality:

> *This delicate balance between teacher and students is a 'near mystery' of democratic practice, according to Friere, who suggests that teachers have to lead the class with a democratic learning process as well as with critical ideas. 'They must affirm themselves without thereby disaffirming their students.' (p. 30)*

If teachers are to do this then they must be led in the same spirit so that leadership and learning become a pervasive norm and schools become learning organisations in which the processes of leading and learning are mutually supportive and reinforcing.

References

Advisory Committee on the Supply and Education of Teachers (1984) *Report of the Teacher Training Sub-Committee*, London: HMSO.

Advisory Committee on the Supply and Training of Teachers (1978) *Making INSET Work*, London: HMSO.

Advisory Conciliation and Arbitration Service (1986) *Teachers Dispute, ACAS Independent Panel, Report of the Appraisal Working Group*, London: ACAS.

Alfonso, R. and Goldsberry, L. (1982) 'Colleagueship in Supervision', in Sergiovanni (1982).

Argyris, C. and Schön, D. (1974) *Theory in Practice*, San Francisco, CA: Jossey Bass.

Barber, M. (1997) *The Learning Game*, London: Indigo.

Barth, R.S. (1990) *Improving Schools From Within*, San Francisco, CA: Jossey Bass.

Bayne-Jardine, C. and Holly, P. (1994) *Developing Quality Schools*, London: Falmer Press.

Belbin, M. (1981) *Management Teams: Why They Succeed or Fail*, Oxford: Heinemann.

Bell, L. and Day, C. (1991) *Managing the Professional Development of Teachers*, Buckingham: Open University Press.

Bennett, N., Glatter, R., Levaciá, R. (1994) *Improving Educational Management Through Research and Consultancy*, London: Paul Chapman Publishing.

Bennis, W. and Nanus, B. (1985) *Leaders*, New York: Harper & Row.

Berger, P. and Luckman, T. (1996) *Social Construction Reality: A Treatise in the Sociology of Knowledge*, New York: Doubleday.

Blumberg, A. (1980) *Supervisors and Teachers*, Berkeley, CA: McCutchan.

Bottery, M. (1994) *Lessons For Schools*, London: Cassell.

Bowring-Carr, C. and West-Burnham, J. (1997) *Effective Learning in Schools*, London: Pitman.

Burns, J.M. (1978) *Leadership*, New York: Harper.

Calderhead, J. and Gates, P. (1993) *Conceptualizing Reflection in Teacher Development*, London: Falmer Press.

Caldwell, B. (1997) 'Thinking in Time: A Gestalt for Schools of the New Millennium', in Davies and Ellison (1997).

Caldwell, B. and Spinks, J. (1988) *The Self Managing School*, London: Falmer Press.

Capra, F. (1997) *The Web of Life: A New Synthesis of Mind and Matter*, London: Flamingo.

Chelimsky, E. (1985) 'Old Patterns and New Directions in Program Evaluation', in Chelimsky, E. (ed.), *Program Evaluation: Patterns and Directions*, Washington DC: APSA.

Claxton, G. (1996) 'Integrated learning theory and the learning teacher', in Claxton, G. *et al.* (1996).

Claxton, G., Atkinson, T., Osborn, M. and Wallace, M. (1996) *Liberating the Learner*, London: Routledge.

Cohen, L. and Manion, C. (1980) *Research Methods in Education*, London: Croom Helm.

Cooper, R. (1986) 'Managing INSET: Learning from TRIST', unpublished paper delivered to the Welsh Collaborative Project Conference on 'Core Themes for Schools/Colleges focused INSET', Llandrindod, Powys.

Covey, S. (1989) *The Seven Habits of Highly Effective People*, London: Simon & Schuster.

Csikszentmihalyi, M. and Rathorde, K. (1990) 'The psychology of wisdom', in Sternberg (1990).

Darling-Hammond, L. (1997) *The Right To Learn*, San Francisco, CA: Jossey Bass.

Davies, B. and Ellison, L. (1997) *School Leadership for the 21st Century*, London: Routledge.

Deming, W.E. (1983) *Out of the Crisis*, Cambridge MA: MIT.

Department of Education and Science (1972) *Teacher Education and Training*, London: HMSO.

Department of Education and Science (1974) *In-Service Education and Training: Some Considerations*, London: HMSO.

Department of Education and Science (1983) *Teaching Quality*, London: HMSO.

Department of Education and Science (1985) *Better Schools*, London: HMSO.

Department of Education and Science (1986) *The LEA Training Grants Scheme*, Circular 6/86, London: HMSO.

Dewey, J. (1909) *How We Think*, Boston, MA: Heath.

Dewey, J. (1929) *The Sources of a Science of Education*, New York: Liveright.

Dori, Y. (1995) 'Co-operative development of chemistry computer assisted instruction by experts, teachers and students', *Journal of Science Education and Technology*, 4(2), 163–70.

Douglas, B. (1991) 'Teachers as experts: a case study of school-based staff development', in Bell and Day (1991).

Drucker, P. (1988) *Management*, Oxford: Heinemann.

Drucker, P. (1993) *Post-Capitalist Society*, New York: HarperCollins.

Earley, P. (1977) 'School development planning and target setting', *Leading Edge*, 1(2), September, 18.

Earley, P. (1992) *The School Management of Competences Project*, Crawley: School Management South.

Earley, P. (1997) 'Target Setting', *Leading Edge*, London: London Leadership Centre.

Evans, A. and Tomlinson, J. (1989) *Teacher Appraisal: A Nationwide Approach*, London: Jessica Kingsley.

Everard, K. (1990) 'The competency approach to management development', *Management in Education* 4(2).

Fidler, B. and Cooper, R. (eds) (1988) *Staff Appraisal in Schools and Colleges*, Harlow: Longman.

Fukuyama, F. (1995) *TRUST: The Social Virtues and the Creation of Prosperity*, London: Hamish Hamilton.

Fullan, M. (1982) *The Meaning of Educational Change*, New York: Teachers College Press.

Fullan, M. (1993) *Change Forces*, London: Falmer Press.

Fullan, M. and Hargreaves, A. (1992) *What's Worth Fighting For In Your School?*, Buckingham: Open University Press.

Gardner, H. (1984) *Frames of Mind*, London: Fontana.

Gardner, H. (1993) *Multiple Intelligences: The Theory in Practice*, New York: Basic Books.

Gardner, H. (1997) 'Opening Minds', in Mulgan (ed.) (1997).

Garratt, B. (1990) *Creating a Learning Organisation: A Guide to Leadership, Learning and Development*, Cambridge: Director Books.

Geva-May, I. and Dori, Y. (1996) 'Analysis of an induction model', *British Journal of In-service Education*, 22(3), 335–56.

Gibbs, G. (1992) *Improving the Quality of Student Learning*, Bristol: Technical and Educational Services.

Giroux, H.A. (1988) *Teachers As Intellectuals*, New York: Bergin & Garvey.

Glover, D. and Law, S. (1996) *Managing Professional Development in Education*, London: Kogan Page.

Graham, J. (1996) 'The Teacher Training Agency, confirming professional development policy and the definition of competencies for serving teachers', *British Journal of In-Service Education*, 22(2), 121–32.

Hague, D. (1997) 'Transforming the dinosaurs' in Mulgan (ed.) (1997).

Hall, V. (1996) 'When the going gets tough: learning through a taught doctorate programme', in Claxton *et al.* (1996).

Hall, V., Cromey-Hawke, N. and Oldroyd, D. (1996) *Management Self-Development: A School Distance Learning Programme*, Bristol: NDCEMP.

Hammer, M. and Champy, J. (1993) *Reengineering the Corporation: A Manifesto for Business Revolution*, London: Nicholas Brearley.

Handy, C. (1985) *Gods of Management*, London: Pan.

Handy, C. (1986) *Understanding Organisations*, Harmondsworth: Penguin.

Handy, C. (1989) *The Age of Unreason*, London: Hutchinson.

Handy, C. (1994) *Understanding Organisations*, 4th edn, London: Penguin.

Hare, W. (1993) *What Makes A Good Teacher*, Ontario Althouse Press.

Hargreaves, A. (1995) 'Beyond collaboration: critical teacher development in the post modern age', in Smyth (ed.) (1995).

Hargreaves, D.H. (1997) 'Education' in Mulgan (ed.) (1997).

Hargreaves, D. and Hopkins, D. (1991) *The Empowered School: The Management and Practice of Development Planning*, London: Cassell.

Her Majesty's Inspectorate/Department of Education and Science (1976) 'Yellow Book', unpublished brief to the Prime Minister's Office in advance of the Ruskin College speech, cited in Ball, S.J. (1990) *Politics and Policy Making in Education: Explorations in Policy Sociology*, London: Routledge.

Hitchcock, G. and Hughes, D. (1995) *Research and the Teacher*, 2nd edn, London: Routledge.

Holly, P. (1994) 'Striving for congruence: the properties of a learning system', in Bayne-Jardine and Holly (1994).

Honey, P. and Mumford, A. (1986) *Using Your Learning Style*, Maidenhead: Peter Honey.

Honey, P. and Mumford, A. (1986) *The Manual of Learning Styles*, Maidenhead: Peter Honey.

Hopkins, D., Ainscow, M. and West, M. (1994) *School Improvement in an Era of Change*, London: Cassell.

Huczynski, A. (1983) *Encyclopaedia of Management Development Methods*, Aldershot: Gower.

Hughes, P. and Jones, J. (1994) 'Managing teacher appraisal: an exercise in collaboration', *British Journal of In-service Education*, 20(2), 209–12.

Illich, I. (1971) *Deschooling Society*, Harmondsworth: Penguin.

Johnson, G. and Scholes, K. (1993) *Exploring Corporate Strategy*, 3rd edn, Hemel Hempstead: Prentice-Hall.

Jones, J. (1993) *Appraisal and Staff Development in Schools*, London: David Fulton.

Jones, J. and O'Sullivan, F. (1997) 'Energising middle management', in Tomlinson (ed.) (1997).

Joyce, B. and Showers, B. (1988) *Student Achievement Through Staff Development*, Harlow: Longman.

Juran, J. (1979) *Quality Control Handbook*, 3rd edn, New York: McGraw Hill.

Kelly, M. (1995) 'Turning heads: changes in the preferred learning styles of school leaders and managers in the 1990s', *School Organisation*, 15(2), 189–201.

Knowles, J.G. (1993) 'Life-history accounts as mirrors', in Calderhead and Gates (1993).

Kolb, D. (1984) *Experiential Learning: Experience as the Source of Learning and Development*, Englewood Cliffs, NJ: Prentice-Hall.

Lawler, E. (1992) *The Ultimate Advantage: Creating the High Involvement Organisation*, San Francisco, CA: Jossey Bass.

Leavitt, H. (1965) 'Applied organisational change in industry', in March, J. (ed.) (1965) *Handbook of Organisations*, Skokie, IL: Rand McNally.

Lepani, B. (1994) *The new learning society the challenge for schools,* University of Sydney Seminar Series No. 33, May 1994, University of Sydney.

Lewin, K. (1946) 'Action research and minority problems', *Journal of Social Issues*, 2.

Little, J. (1982) 'Norms of collegiality and experimentation', *American Educational Research Journal*, 19(3).

Lomax, P. (1994) 'Action research for managing change', in Bennett *et al.* (1994).

Lyons, G. (1976) *Heads' Tasks: A Handbook of Secondary School Administration*, Slough: NFER.

McGill, I. and Beaty, L. (1995) *Action Learning*, 2nd edn, London: Kogan Page.

McNiff J. (1988) *Action Research: Principles and Practice*, London: Macmillan.

Manguel, A. (1997) *A History of Reading*, London: Flamingo.

Miles, M. (1987) *Practical Guidelines for School Administrators: How to Get There*, paper presented at the Effective Schools Programs and the Urban High School Symposium, AERA Annual Meeting, Washington, DC.

Mintzberg, H. (1994) *The Rise and Fall of Strategic Planning*, London: Prentice Hall.

Mor, D. (1989) *An Induction Program*, Ministry of Education and Culture, Jerusalem.

Morgan, G. (1986) *Images of Organisations*, London: Sage.

Mulgan, G. (ed.) (1997) *Life After Politics*, London: Fontana.

Mumford, A. (1994) *Learning Styles and Learning Designs*, BEMAS (Conference Address), Manchester.

Naisbitt, J. and Aburdene, P. (1990) *Megatrands 2000*, London: Pan.

National Commission for Education (NEC) (1996) *Success Against the Odds*, London: Routledge.

Noble, P, and Pym, R. (1970) 'Collegial authority and the receding locus of power', *British Journal of Sociology*.

Oakland, J.S. (1993) *Total Quality Management*, 2nd edn, Oxford: Butterworth-Heinemann.

Organization for Economic Cooperation and Development (1975) *Education Development Strategy in England and Wales*, Paris: OECD.

O'Sullivan F, (1995) 'The role of collaborative evaluation in supporting self managing schools', *British Journal of In-Service Education*, 20(3), 371–85.

Oxford Consortium for Educational Achievement (1996) *Thinking towards a Coherent Approach to Monitoring in Education*, Old Woodhouse: OCEA.

Pedler, M., Burgoyne, J. and Boydell, T. (1987) *The Learning Company*, Maidenhead: McGraw-Hill.

Perkins, D. (1992) *Smart Schools*, New York: Free Press.

Peters, T. and Waterman, R. (1982) *In Search of Excellence*, New York: Harper & Row.

Pollard, A. and Tann, S. (1993) *Reflective Teaching in the Primary School: A Handbook for the Classroom*, 2nd edn, London: Cassell.

Quinn, R., Faerman, S., Thompson, M. and McGrath, M. (1996) *Becoming a Master Manager: A Competency Framework*, 2nd edn, New York: Wiley.

Reid, M.A. and Barrington, H. (1997) *Training Interviews*, London: Institute of Personnel and Development.

Reynolds, D. and Cuttance, P. (eds) (1992) *School Effectiveness: Research, Policy and Practice*, London: Cassell.

Rosenholtz, S. J. (1991) *Teacher's Workplace*, New York: Teachers College Press.

Said, E.W. (1994) *Representations of the Intellectual*, New York: Vintage Books.

Sammons, P., Hillman, J. and Mortimore, P. (1995) *Key Characteristics of Effective Schools*, London: OFSTED.

Saville and Holdsworth (1995) *Best Practice in the Use of Job Analysis Techniques*, Thames Ditton, Surrey: SHL.

Schön, D. (1987) *Educating the Reflective Practitioner*, San Francisco, CA: Jossey Bass.

Scriven, M. (1967) 'The methodology of evaluation', in Stake (ed.) (1967).

Senge, P. (1990) *The Fifth Discipline*, New York: Doubleday.

Sergiovanni, T. (1982) *Supervision of Teaching*, Alexandria: ASCD.

Sergiovanni, T. (1996) *Leadership for the Schoolhouse*, San Francisco, CA: Jossey Bass.

Shor, J. (1993) 'Education in politics: Paulo Frieve's critical pedagory', in McLaren, P. and Leonard, P. (1993) *Paulo Frieve: A Critical Encounter*, London: Routledge.

Skilbeck, M. (1970) *Dewey*, London: Collier Macmillan.

Skinner, B.F. (1969) *Contingencies and Reinforcement*, New York: Applebaum.

Smyth, J. (ed.) (1995) *Critical Discourse on Teacher Development*, London: Cassell.

Stake, R. (ed.) (1967) *Curriculum Evaluation*, Chicago, I: Rand McNally.

Sternberg, R.J. (1990) *Wisdom*, Cambridge: Cambridge University Press.

Stoll, L. and Fink, D. (1996) *Changing Our Schools*, Buckingham: Open University Press.

Strauss, A. and Corbin, J. (1990) *Basics of Qualitative Research: Grounded Theory Procedures and Techniques*, Newbury Park, CA: Sage.

Stufflebeam, D., Foley, W., Gephart, W. and Guba, E., Hammond, R., Merriman, H. and Provus, M. (1971) *Educational Evaluation and Decision Making*, Itasca, MN: Peacock.

Swieringa, J. and Wierdsma, A. (1992) *Becoming a Learning Organization: Beyond the Learning Curve*, Wokingham: Addison-Wesley.

TAIPAN UK, (1995) *1995–2005: 13 Trends and Events that will Rock the World* (Special Report), London: Fleet Street Publications.

Teacher Training Agency (TTA) (1996) *Standards and a National Professional Qualification for Subject Leaders; Training for Serving Headteachers*, Consultation Papers, London: TTA.

Teacher Training Agency (1997a) *National Standards for Headteachers*, London: TTA.

Teacher Training Agency (1997b) *National Standards for Subject Leaders* (revised draft), London: TTA.

Tennant, M. (1997) *Psychology and Adult Learning*, London: Routledge.

Tomlinson, H. (ed.) (1997) *Managing Continuing Professional Development in Schools*, London: Paul Chapman Publishing.

Turner, G. and Clift, P. (1988) *Studies in Teacher Appraisal*, Lewes: Falmer Press.

Veugelers, W. and Zijlstra, H. (1995) 'Learning together: in-service education in networks of schools', *British Journal of In-service Education*, 21(1), 37–48.

Vygotsky, L.S. (1962) *Thought and Language*, Cambridge MA: Harvard University Press.

Vygotsky, L.S. (1978) *Mind in Society*, Cambridge MA: Harvard University Press.

Wallace, M. (1991) *School-centred Management Training*, London: Paul Chapman Publishing.

Wallace, M. (1996) 'When is experiential learning not learning?', in Claxton *et al.* (1996).

West-Burnham, J. (1997) *Managing Quality in Schools*, 2nd edn, London: Pitman.

Wheatley, M.J. (1992) *Leadership and the New Science*, San Francisco, CA: Berrett-Koehler.

Whetten, D., Cameron, K. and Woods, M. (1994) *Developing Management Skills for Europe*, London: HarperCollins.

REFERENCES

White, P., Hodgson, P. and Crainer, S. (1996) *The Future of Leadership: Riding the Rapids to the 21st Century*, London: Pitman.

Wragg, E.C., Wikeley, F.J., Wragg, C.M. and Haynes, G.S. (1996) *Teacher Appraisal Observed*, London: Routledge.

Index

■ ■ ■